S0-ALM-532

FRILANDSMUSEET

THE OPEN-AIR MUSEUM
Department of The National Museum

ENGLISH GUIDE

TEXT: KAI ULDALL
WITH ADDITIONS BY PETER MICHELSEN AND
BJARNE STOKLUND
TRANSLATION: JOHN HIGGS
ILLUSTRATED BY FRODE KIRK

THE NATIONAL MUSEUM
COPENHAGEN
DENMARK
1991

About the Museum...

Frilandsmuseet (The Open-Air Museum) is a department of the National Museum of Denmark. It is a collection of old farmsteads, cottages, mills etc. which have been brought from their original sites in different parts of Denmark and the former Danish provinces of Southern Sweden and South Schleswig. The buildings have been transferred from their home districts to a natural environment in a rural park and are equipped with traditional furniture, utensils and implements. The Museum, therefore, gives a picture of old Danish country homes as they existed through the ages in different geographical areas and under different economic conditions. Most of the buildings show the homes of farmers and smallholders but you can also see in the park the homes of the seafarer, the fisherman, the miller and the village craftsman.

The purpose of the museum is to portray the living conditions of the countryman; to show the houses and homes and the farms equipped with the implements that would have been used. There are, therefore, no displays or showcases like those in a normal indoor museum, nor any labels to explain the many items of equipment. The buildings are labelled and numbered; descriptions of them and their contents will be found in this guide.

It should be pointed out that it is not always possible to give an exact date for any particular building. Even if it is known when the original building was put up, there have often been many modifications and alterations over the years which have substantially altered the original character.

In the gardens of the houses old varieties of flowering plants and fruit trees have been planted.

Frilandsmuseet contains only rural buildings; town buildings will be found at **Den Gamle By**, Århus.

ISBN 87-89384-06-7

1. FISHERMAN'S COTTAGE FROM AGGER,
NORTH SEA COAST

The home district of this cottage was the open coast of North Jutland where storms and sand drifts hindered farming and made it im-
possible to build harbours. This cottage is a "longhouse"° with farm
buildings in the eastern end and the dwelling-house in the western.
The roof has a turf ridge.° Note the louver° or smoke hole instead of
a chimney. The building is of half-timbered° construction and much
of the wood used for this is thin; the uprights are placed directly on
the stone sill. Most of the timber is from wrecks washed up on the
beach and the walls are partly filled with beach stone and partly
with wattle° and daub and some bricks.° The cottage consists of a
nave and narrow side aisles, i.e. the rows of inner posts carried the
roof which on both sides projects over the narrow aisles or outshots.
The main beams are mortised through the inner posts. Only at the
gable end, and to make room for the windows in the two dwelling
rooms, is there no outshot. South of the cottage is a winch well.°

*Mangle° board
and roller*

The door near the western gable leads into a small cobbled entry.
To the left a door opens into the "best° room", which has in it a chest
and wardrobe containing textiles. This room cannot be heated and
was only used for parties and other gatherings. In the northern out-
shot° is an alcove° bed for guests and a hand° mill. This part of the
house is a later addition.

Milking stool

Straw° basket

Wool winder

Skein winder

Back creel

Crusie° lamp

From the entry the door to the right opens into the clay-floored room which served as living-room, dining-room and bedroom. The fixed benches and long table at which the family took their meals are near the windows. As was customary among peasants the master sat at the head of the table and the sons and servants were placed according to rank upon the long bench under the window. The women stood, or sat on a backless seat, on the inner side of the table.

In the walls are a built-in cupboard and alcove° beds. On the iron stove°, which is heated through the wall from the kitchen, is a tray for drying malt and corn. The black Jutland pottery was made by hand without the use of a potter's wheel; other examples will be seen in the larder behind the entry and in the pantry in the southern outshot. A door by the stove leads into the cobbled kitchen which has neither chimney nor ceiling. The fire is built on a raised hearth close to the dividing wall and under the louver° or smoke hole. To the north is the whitewashed bread oven, smoke from which found its way out through the louver. The next room is the original entry where the inner posts and the outshot or side aisles may be seen. Some fishing implements and a back creel are kept here. This original entry divides the dwelling proper from the barn and cow sheds.

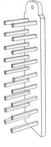

Dish rack

Fish-hook rack

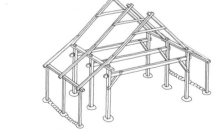

Timber frame with side aisles or outshots°

Jutland° pot

Fish platter

Ember° holder

Candle° holder

2. SKIPPER'S COTTAGE FROM FANØ, NORTH SEA COAST

The inhabitants of the small, sandy and wind-swept island of Fanø were fishermen and sailors. Contact in former days with Holland being strong, the buildings and the furniture of Fanø were influenced by Dutch and Frisian design.

A "longhouse"° with barn, cowshed etc. in the eastern end, and dwelling-house in the western. The walls are built of red brick°.

The rooms of this house resemble those of the house from Rømø (see no. 34). A passage divides the farm buildings from the dwelling-house. On the right in the passage is a small store room containing black Jutland pots and china. The dwelling house contains a winter living-room to the south and a summer living-room and a kitchen to the north. At the far end there are two smaller unheated rooms. The walls are covered partly by Dutch tiles°, some of them depicting the master's ship, and partly by ornamented painted panels. The pictures of ships and some nautical instruments indicate that it is the home of a seafarer.

Warming° pan

Sun-dial

Sheep shears

Wooden° tray

Marline° spike

Bait bucket

3. BUILDINGS FROM THE ISLAND OF BORNHOLM
FARMSTEAD FROM ØSTER LARSKER

Four detached wings set in a rectangle. Most of the buildings probably date from about 1800 but the east wing was built in 1842 and
the bakehouse is from shortly before 1865. It is all half-timbered° and
the dwelling-house is partly built on ground° plates; the tie° beams
are mortised through the uprights. The black timber is oak supple-
mented with elm, ash and pine, the in-filling whitewashed as the
ground° sill.

Excavations on the original site have uncovered predecessors of
the dwelling-house, part of which was made broader by addition of
a lean-to° in the period 1852–65. At the same time the scullery° was
placed outside the house in the detached bakehouse in the garden.

Hurricane
lantern

Jar for preserves

Fly-net

The entrance farthest from the gateway leads to a passage with the maidservant's bedchamber and two larders to one side. Opposite is the living-room for everyday use and furnished with folding° bed, table and chairs, and a grandfather clock. Beside this room is the kitchen where the cooking took place at an iron range. Behind is the bedchamber which together with the kitchen is installed in the broader part of the dwelling-house. Through the living-room to a middle room with desk, divan, table, chairs and another grandfather clock. This room was more private than the living-room where the servants came in to eat together with the family. Both rooms can be heated by an iron stove°. So is the case in the next room which has windows to both sides. This parlour is decorated with wallpaper with large flowers and provided with upholstered furniture and carpet on the floor. The furnishing of these rooms belongs to the style of the first quarter of the 20th century.

Ladle

Pail

The entrance to the other part of the dwelling-house is from the courtyard upstairs a flight of stone steps just inside the gateway. This end of the dwelling-house has its height because – as is often the case on the island of Bornholm – the farmstead is lying on sloping ground. From the lobby the parlour can be seen from the other side. Through an intermediate room and past a spare bedroom the best° room or hall is reached. The furnishing of these rooms is more old fashioned than the everyday rooms. The hall has been used for storage and feast. Many chairs are kept in reserve along the walls. The room has windows in the high gable and under the hall there is a spacious cellar°.

In the wing with the gateway there is a farmhands' room and a mangling-room. On the other side of the gateway is a workshop and then follow floors for winnowing and threshing, a barn and a coach-house. At the end of the wing a privy has been added. In the south wing are rooms for smaller livestock, a cowshed, and barns. The west wing contains gateway, barn, threshing floor, a stable with a harness room, and a pigsty.

Hanging lamp

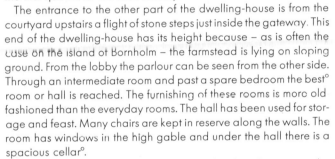

Thresher

Winnowing-machine

In the courtyard is a dunghill, a sweep well° with a well-curb of sandstone dated 1831. In front of the dwelling-house is a small garden behind a picket fence. Here among other things fig and mulberry. Outside the west gable of the dwelling-house a place for firewood. Around the gable is the small bakehouse with an open° chimney and a bread° oven. The passage between the bakehouse and the kitchen leads to the garden where there is another well with a sandstone well-curb, this one dating from the year 1829.

Shovel for winnowing

Chaff-cutter

WATERMILL FROM PEDERSKER

The half-timbering° of the small house is creosoted black while the infilling, which is partly brick° and partly sandstone, is white-washed. The uprights rest directly on the stones of the ground° sill. The beams are mortised through the upright posts. These joints are strengtened internally with brackets.

As usual in Bornholm the bottom lath of the roof is resting on hori-zontal wooden pegs driven into the side of the wall° plate. – The water drives a big undershot wheel beneath the gable. The power is transferred through simple gearing to the upper stone of the mill. – The watermill was originally situated on a stream a little below the farm, to which it belonged.

4. FARMSTEAD FROM OSTENFELD, SOUTH SCHLESWIG

The building is composed of a nave° which forms one large room and two side aisles. It is half-timbered° filled in with yellow bricks°. The walls of the rear part of the house, however, which include the sitting-rooms, are whitewashed clay and were a later addition. The roof is thatched and has a turf ridge°. This type of building is common in northwest Germany and a few were to be found in South Schleswig which until 1864 belonged to Denmark. The main nave° of the building is common both to cattle and human beings and has an open hearth at one end. Although this was normal in the Iron Age and early Middle Ages the year 1685 is carved over the entrance. This does not indicate the year the house was built as dendrochronological° dating (i.e. by means of the annual growth rings in the timber) suggests it is a good hundred years older.

The entrance is through large double doors at one end. Over these doors is the name of the owner, Hans Petersen, and the date 1685. In Denmark it was normal for dwelling-houses to be built east to west but it was common for these houses to be built with their main entrance on to the village street. The building has no chimney. Inside, under the thick sooty beams, the one large room with clay floor common both to humans and animals also served as the threshing floor. Hay and straw were stored in the loft where it was kept dry by the heat and smoke from the hearth below.

Carriage steps

Curfew°

Curfew°

Foot° warmer

As you enter, the threshing floor is immediately in front of you. On the floor are two carriages. The cattle were kept in the stalls behind the uprights which carry the roof; they faced inwards unlike the Danish practice which was to yoke them facing the outer wall. On the left, close to the door, is the stable. Further on, by the righthand side door, is a bread oven without a chimney. The rear end of the nave° was used to live in. The chairs stand round the open hearth. The smoke from the fire found its way out of the doors or through a small opening in the southern gable. Over the hearth hangs a cooking pot. To the left is a hanging shelf for bread, etc. By the gable wall is a raised platform for kitchen utensils and over that are hung dishes and a brass sconce or candle° holder. In front of the windows in the aisles are recesses with tables, seats and alcove° beds. The bed curtains are of a special Schleswig double cloth. On one of the tables is a mangle board with a roller. The two furthest rooms were added later to the original house. The left hand room is a sitting-room with the year 1787 and Frisian tiles° on some of the walls; it also has alcove° beds and an iron stove fired through the wall. From this room there is a spy window to the nave. The right-hand room is the "best° room" for festivals and it has wooden panelling carved in the renaissance style and solid fixed benches on the clay floor. Some of the window panes are decorated with etched paintings, ornaments, and names. It was the custom for guests at a house-warming party to present window panes of this type to their host. The cupboards and chests were carved by the local craftsmen in late gothic and renaissance style.

Waffle iron

Baby's bottle

Crusie° lamp

Clothes drying rack

Pyramid° shelves

Timber frame with side aisles or outshots°

Bread rack

5. FUGLEVAD WINDMILL

(No admission)

This is a "Dutch" or "tower" mill, built on this same site in 1832 and in use here until 1906. This type of windmill, in which only the cap carrying the sails was turned to the wind, was introduced into Denmark in the 18th century, but was not common until later when it displaced the post-mill (see nos. 9 and 74). The cap was turned from the balcony of the mill. The mill house is covered with shingles and the bottom walls are brick.

It was once common to find, as here, two mills situated close to each other; the windmill set high on a hill and the watermill in the valley bottom where there was a stream. The way down to the watermill was often steep and when heavy horse wagons laden with grain went down to the Funen watermill (no. 6) a dragshoe was used as a brake.

Dragshoe for braking horse wagon

6. WATERMILL FROM ELLESTED, FUNEN

A "longhouse"° with a dormer on each side and a wing towards the garden. The eastern end of the building contains the mill and the remainder is the dwelling house. The building is of half-timbered° construction with joists mortised through the uprights in the eastern part, the timber of which according to dendrochronology° was felled 1776/77. The tie° beams are placed on top of the wall° plate in the rest of the building which also dates from the eighteenth century though there have been alterations since then. The timber is reddish brown with yellow-washed brick. The wing and the southern wall of the mill are whitewashed and the eastern gable is boarded.

Toll cup for the miller's share of the grain

Toy trumpet

Table lamp

Plant stand

At the eastern end are two overshot wheels to which the water from the pond passes through a wooden sluice which can be regulated by boards on the end of poles through the gable end. There is another sluice for the surplus water which is regulated from outside.

The wheel furthest from the mill pond drives a horizontal crown wheel under the ceiling which in turn drives a kibbling mill near the gable and a fast rotating shell mill out of sight under the floor; both of them are used for producing barley groats. In addition it drives a grading machine and a grain cleaner near the stairs. Also in the corner near the door to the garden is a rye mill sometimes used for wheat. The wheel nearer the mill pond drives a gear system which in turn drives a vertical shaft which works the upper millstone; the same wheel also works the lift which conveys the ground meal from the mill to the flour sieve or boulter in the big wooden box standing against the wall at the back. In the boulter is a rotating roller covered with a very fine linen cloth. Below the floor near the stairs to the basement is an oat crusher which at a later date was added to the drive system of this wheel. Between the mill and the boulter is a rope sack hoist to take sacks up to the loft, which can also be reached by the stairs. From the loft grain can be fed into the mills through shutes. Along the sides of the loft the sacks are stacked, each one marked with the initials of a customer; they are arranged according to the order in which they are collected by the driver. There are also bushels for measuring corn by volume.

Shaving mirror

A staircase leads from the mill through an entry to the dwelling house, the interior of which is furnished as it was in the last decade of the nineteenth century. In the mill room is the miller's desk. Near the window are benches and a table; there are also a grandfather clock, a cooking stove and an alcove° bed for the maid. In the corner by the door to the kitchen is a place for children to play. In the kitchen an iron range has been put in the former open° chimney. At the end of the kitchen are a dark beer room with preserving jars on the shelves and a larder. At the other end of the kitchen is a door leading to a bedroom. In the middle of the nineteenth century special rooms for sleeping became common instead of the older arrangement of alcove° beds in the living room. From the bedroom a door

Holder for newspapers

Stewpan

Pail

leads to the parlour which has wallpaper and the floor painted with a star pattern, upholstered furniture, bric-á-brac, pot plants and window curtains; the occasional chairs have white antimacassars to protect them from hair oil. Going back through the kitchen, the scullery° is in the transverse wing. There are a kneading trough, brewing vat, stewing pan, and sundry other utensils. The bench° and table originally came from the mill room. There is an open° chimney from which the big oven can be stoked and two brewing coppers, one fixed° and one movable. In the corner of the scullery° is a milk room with a stove which could be used to protect the milk against the frost; it was originally in one of the living rooms. A door leads into the garden from which is the entrance to the woodshed behind the oven at the end of the wing; stacks of firewood are arranged by the millpond. Also in the garden which is of late nineteenth century style are two tables made from millstones.

Re-enter the dwelling house by the door from the garden past a spare bedroom into the hall from which there is a further view of the parlour. From the hall a door leads to the "best° room" which contains furniture of different periods. There is upholstered furniture, a rocking chair, a wicker chair, bric-á-brac, pot plants and curtains; beyond is a guest bedroom. Returning to the hall the stairs lead to the loft containing chests for storing bedclothes and clothing, a table chest, mangle and toys. Leading from the loft is the daughter's room with a dressing table and a bed which was made by a local journeyman apprentice as a test piece on finishing his apprenticeship. In the dormer overlooking the garden is a guest bedroom.

Whip stretched
by a bottle

Dough trough

Brewing vat

7. BOUNDARY STONE FROM LØVE, CENTRAL JUTLAND

A granite pillar used for marking the boundary of the royal hunting ground. Under the crown is the initial C of the king, Christian VI, the date 1743 and S.D. (standing for Skanderborg District) no. 10.

A short distance behind the boundary stone is a **compartment stone** from a wood near Ganløse, Zealand.

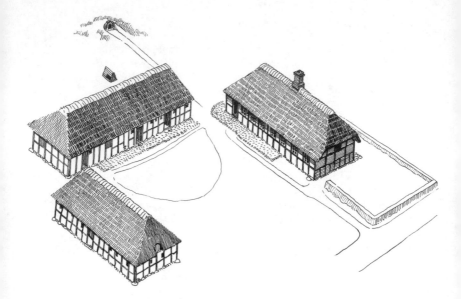

8. FARMSTEAD FROM KARUP HEATH, CENTRAL JUTLAND

Block° for shaping woollen underpants

At one time the farmers on the Jutland heath lived in poor conditions, their buildings being very crude and primitive. For want of timber and clay the walls were built of peat or heather turf and big stones but hovels of this type have long since disappeared. This building, of about 1850, is one of the oldest and simplest now to be found. There is a dwelling-house and two sets of farm buildings which are built of rather crude half-timbered° work. The upright posts stand directly upon the stone sill. The walls are built partly of ordinary and partly of sun-dried° bricks. The thatch of the hipped-roofs is composed of alternate layers of straw and heather and the ridge is covered with turf. The floors are of clay. The bread° oven is situated away from the house to the west. It is in the open but is covered with earth. A dike of heather turf surrounds the small wind swept garden behind the dwelling-house.

Baby-walker°

Sewing cushion

Dead-fall mousetrap

A small cobbled entry at the west end of the dwelling-house leads into the sitting-room which contains an iron stove° bearing the monogram of Christian VI and the date 1735. The room is particularly roomy and the table in front of the fixed benches° under the windows is very long to make room for "knitting festivals". Many sheep were kept on the Jutland heath and there was an important domestic knitting industry. It was customary for men as well as women to meet in different homes in the district in turn on winter evenings. They all worked round the long table and during the evening sang songs and narrated old legends and stories. As was customary the master's seat is at the end of the table and on the wall above are hung framed paper memorials to members of the family who have died; the beds are built-in. Behind the entry is a pantry. To the right of the stove a door opens into a small room which leads into another containing a folding° bed. The door to the left of the stove leads into the kitchen where there is some black Jutland° pottery. – The western building contains the stable, cowshed, threshing floor and barn. In the southern are sheds for fuel, wagons etc.

Biscuit-iron

Horse over-shoe

Rush ox collar

Numbers 8, 9, 22, 29, 30 and 34 come from the less fertile districts of Denmark. Large areas of central Jutland, which are now mostly cultivated, or planted with fir and pine trees were, less than a century ago, open heathland (no. 8). Northeast of Jutland, in the Kattegat, is the wind-swept and sandy island of Læsø (no. 9). In contrast to the eastern part of Jutland, which is relatively sheltered and fertile, much of the western coast is barren and lies exposed to storms which also cause drifting sand (nos. 1 and 34). The coast of southwest Jutland and Schleswig, however, is fertile marsh country protected by a row of sheltering islands (no. 31).

Heather cutter

Fox trap

Scythe° sharpening bench

Wagon seat

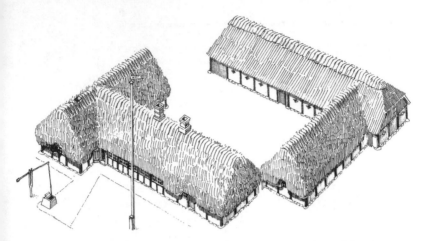

9. FARMSTEAD FROM THE ISLAND OF LÆSØ
IN THE KATTEGAT

Currier's° iron

Decoy° swan

The steading is made up of four wings, only parts of which are joined. The dwelling house is T-shaped and is half-timbered° and whitewashed. The north wing is dated 1736 while the main wing is built a little later. The walls are filled with wattle° and daub, but parts have been repaired later with bricks° taken from a ruined medieval church. The north wall under the windows is timbered with heavy horizontal oak° boards between uprights. (See nos. 37–40, 54 and 55). The uprights are tarred and placed directly on the stone sill. – The thick roof is covered with seaweed.

The door near the south end of the west wall leads into a narrow scullery° with a fixed° copper and a hand° mill in the little room beyond. Through the door on the left is a room with a small raised open hearth and a bread° oven at the rear. The next room is the kitchen which has a larger raised open fireplace with a small flue behind it which heats the iron stoves° in the other rooms. Then follows the dwelling-room° which is panelled and has an iron stove°. Under the windows to the west are the fixed benches° and the long table and by the eastern wall an alcove° bed for the master and his wife. Between the iron stove° and the grandfather clock a door

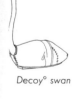

Cheese grater
om the Netherlands

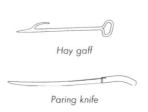

Hay gaff

Paring knife

Milk pitcher

leads into a smaller chamber also with an iron stove° and an alcove° bed. In the dwelling-room° the door to the right of the built-in desk leads into the larders.

To the left of the desk another door opens to a small entry with an outer door. Then follows the northern wing dated 1736. Here is a "best° room" with painted wooden panelling, an alcove° bed for guests or lodgers and a gaily painted chest° of drawers. As the "best° room" on Læsø was often let to shipwrecked people or sailors, there is an iron stove° and behind it a small kitchen. In this kitchen there is a raised hearth without a chimney, the smoke finding its way out through the louver° or smoke-hole in the roof. To the east of the "best° room" there is a bedroom. – From the courtyard at the eastern side of the building is an entrance to the workshop° and in the southern end of the dwelling-house a fuel store which also contains a clinker-built° boat.

The barn and cowshed are in the L-shaped building at the other side of the courtyard. The cowshed to the south is an old building which was extended 1847. The eastern wing is the barn which dates back to about 1880 and never had a seaweed roof.

To the north is a small garden surrounded by a turf bank. To the west is a sweep well° and at some distance a small post mill only for farm use. The sails were covered with light wooden battens instead of the canvas which was used at a later period (see no. 74).

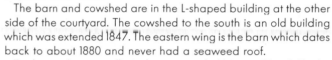

Post mill

Caulking tools

Rattle

Fishing line twister

15–19. BUILDINGS FROM THE FAEROE ISLANDS
IN THE ATLANTIC

15. FARMHOUSE FROM MÚLA ON THE ISLAND
OF BORÐOY

Fishing line twisters

Wool comb for worsted

A "longhouse"° built in 1866 with a dwelling at one end and quarters for animals at the other. The house, which is built half-way down a steep slope has wooden walls at the southern end but the northern is built of stones with turf between; the roof is of turf laid on birch bark.

The entrance is through a small entry which leads on the left into a small kitchen with the "best° room" beyond. This room is called the "glass-room" because it has real windows which were uncommon in the Faeroes; it contains a table and chairs, some small chests and alcove° beds. The room can be heated by a stove° which is fed from the wood and brick fireplace in the kitchen. Next to the kitchen there is a small larder and a room for storing various tools such as those for making rope; in the window is a game made from sheep bones.

Back through the entry is the "smoke-room" originally the only dwelling-room° in a Faeroe house; it has no ceiling or windows and the light comes through a louver° in the roof. The fireplace was originally in the middle of the floor so that the smoke could find its way out through the louver° but at a later date a wooden chimney has been added at one end of the room; opposite the chimney is a folding table and a chest. At the side of the room are alcove° beds with curtains and in front of them fixed benches° with among other things a spinning wheel, wool combs, and a milk pail with a wooden handle. On the floor is a back-creel containing wool and two stools one of which is made from the thoracic vertebra of a whale. Under the beam hangs a whale oil lamp in an adjustable holder.

The door leads to the cowhouse with stalls for two cows which can be tied up with ropes of plaited wool. Also kept in here are a loom, warping frame, spades and other agricultural tools.

Back creel

16. FOODSTORE FROM VIÐEREJÐE ON THE ISLAND OF VIÐOY

The open-air food store is the most important of the many small houses which go to make up a Faeroe farmstead; the wall at one end is made of loose rubble while the remainder is of wooden slats with air spaces between. The most important foodstuffs in the rather primitive economy of the Faeroes, fish, sheep meat and the meat of the pilot whale were hung here and preserved in the fresh air without the use of salt. The building, which is closed with a wooden lock, is also used as a store. Drying food hangs beneath the beams; there are also barrels, a creel, a fowler's net, whale spears, and fishing floats made from the stomach of pilot whales and calfskin.

Fishing float

17. SPLASHMILL FROM SANDUR ON THE ISLAND OF SANDOY

A small watermill with horizontal blades which was owned in common by a number of farmers (see no. 58) in which they could grind their homegrown barley. Simple mills of this type replaced, in many communities, the older hand° driven mills during the eighteenth and nineteenth centuries.

Near to the sluicegate is a stone with a circular depression in it. On this, using another stone on top, the roots of a plant, potentilla erecta were crushed. The crushed roots were pickled and used for dressing sheepskin for shoes or for oilskins.

The buildings (15–18) together give an impression of a characteristic Faeroe settlement. The enclosing wall marks the limit between the outer field – in which some Faeroe sheep graze – and the inner field where the buildings are situated and a few small animals could be grazed and the cultivated fields where hay and barley are grown; these latter are terraced to assist the run-off of water in wet times.

18. KILN-HOUSE FROM MÚLA ON THE ISLAND OF BORÐOY

The building has walls of stone with turf between and is built into the stone wall of the enclosure; the roof is of turf laid on top of straw.

Grain growing was not very important in the Faeroes but in most of the settlements a little six-rowed barley was grown and was used to make small unleavened loaves which were baked in the embers of the fire. As, in the Faeroe climate, the grain very rarely ripened completely it had to be dried in the fireplace on the "smoke-room" (see no. 15) or in a special kiln-house. The ears were ripped off with an iron comb and the straw was then put on the rack to the left of the door and the ears placed on top. A fire was made in the opening in the partition wall. When it was dry the grain was threshed with clubs on a small wooden floor and winnowed with a wooden trough.

Treshing club on a wooden floor

Close by is a small walled enclosure in which archangelica officinalis could be grown as a vegetable and protected from domestic animals; part of the wall is made from the skulls of pilot whales.

Just beyond the gate in the wall is the old "lifting stone" from Múla with which the men of the settlement proved their strength (no. 19).

19. Lifting stone

20. MILESTONE FROM THE DISTRICT OF
HOLSTEBRO, WESTERN JUTLAND

A granite pillar placed on a small mound. The three small holes in the upper part of the front indicate three quarters of a Danish mile. This type of milestone belongs to a system of surveying Danish roads which was developed at the end of the seventeenth century (see no. 61).

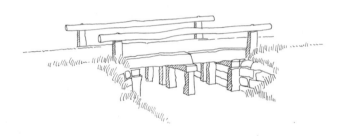

21. BRIDGE FROM SMEDEVAD NEAR HOLSTEBRO,
WESTERN JUTLAND

It is built out of large slabs of granite cut like beams and mainly placed horizontally though the pillars which support the two bays are vertical. The construction is copied from the construction of wooden bridges. – In the Middle Ages roads crossed the rivers at fords and most of the bridges were wooden but a few were of stone. Most of the old bridges which now remain, however, were constructed or altered during road works in the second half of the eighteenth century.

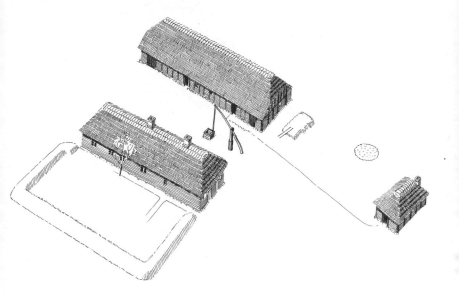

22. FARMSTEAD FROM VEMB, WEST JUTLAND

The steading is made up of two detached parallel wings with a farmyard in the middle and a forge a little to the east. The dwelling house and the barn were built about 1770 with thin pine half-timbering° and no horizontal members between the uprights. The beams are placed directly on the wall° plates. The walls were originally infilled with clay but in the 1820s this was partly replaced by bricks° especially in the south wall of the dwelling house and in part of the north wall of the barn; in some places the bricks are sun-dried°. The roof is thatched with alternating bands of straw and heather.

The door to the dwelling house is at the east end and leads into a cobbled scullery° which has no ceiling; there is an open fireplace with a bread° oven at the back and a fixed° brewing copper to the right. In the scullery° also are a cheese° press and a wooden trivet and in the loft a malt bin° made from straw° and a braiding loom. Next to the chimney is the entrance to a small room in the gable used for storing peat etc.; from here there is a trap door for putting

Candlestick

Mortar

Chopping board and knife

Cheese press°

Peat knife

food into the pigsty. In the small larder behind the scullery° are among other things a kneading trough and a butter churn°. From the scullery° the door leads to the kitchen with its raised open hearth for cooking on. The stoves° in the other rooms are stoked from here. On the hearth are an iron pot and a Jutland° pot for cooking. In front of the chimney the ceiling is raised to form a box-shaped room for storing hams, sausages etc. The dwelling-room° beyond the kitchen, like the other rooms has a clay floor. Under the windows is a long table and fixed bench°; and a loose bench° stands in front of the table. The wall is panelled behind the fixed benches°. Under the beam over the table are some horn spoons. The iron stove° bears a relief of the lion from the Norwegian coat of arms; over it is a rack for drying clothes. There is also a simple armchair. On the walls hang some framed prints with religious motifs and some handwritten wedding congratulations. Opposite the windows is a board wall with doors opening into the alcove° beds. The wall at the back of the beds is partly covered with straw. Between the two beds is a built-in cupboard with two flaps. The door near the stove° leads into a small room which is in the same bay of the house as the kitchen. This room was originally used as a bedroom, sometimes for the widow of the previous farmer; the stove° was made in Norway. By the stove is an armchair made of coiled straw°. The alcove° bed has curtains and part of the back wall is straw covered; by the window is a bench° which can also be used as a bed. On the walls are framed memorials and a sampler. At the opposite end of the dwelling-room° from the stove° is another small room which was used by the house wife for weaving. By the loom is a frame for setting up the warp for the loom; near it stands the box from which the different balls of yarn were led into the frame. Leaving the dwelling-room° through the cobbled entry a door leads to a small bedroom.

Crossing the yard, the barn is entered through the door in the middle; the timber frame with side aisles is made of thin pine wood supported by cross braces. There is no wagon entrance to the barn or the grain store because the sheaves were normally tipped out-

Peat spade

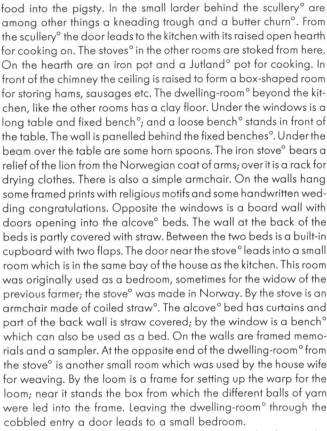

Smith's tong

Beet seeder

Chaff-cutter

side. If there were more sheaves than would go into the store then stacks were often made around the buildings. Westwards from the grain store through a low gateway is a room that was used for a carriage house and workshop°; on the other side of the store is a threshing floor and a fodder floor. In the eastern end of the building is a stall for cows and for oxen used for draught and a pen for sheep.

Outside, by the gable of the barn is a dunghill and in the middle of the yard is a sweep well°. To the south of the dwelling house is a garden enclosed by a turf bank. Between the barn and the forge is a circular area of paving used for storing the clay for making Jutland° pots.

The forge lies a little away to the east and was built about 1870 of simple half-timbering° with brick° in-filling; it was only for farm use. There is an open° chimney with a hearth and bellows for blowing the fire; there is also an anvil and a work bench with a slamp and various tools.

Shuttle

Heddle-block

Creel for
the warp

Loom

Warping mill

Tenderhook

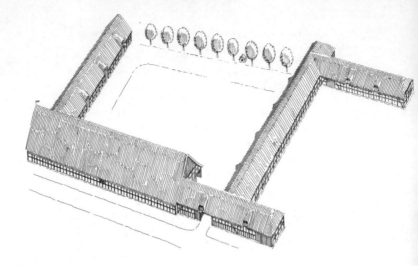

25. OUTBUILDINGS FROM A MANOR HOUSE AT
FJELLERUP, DJURSLAND, EASTERN JUTLAND

Three wings in rectangular form around a cobbled courtyard, at the fourth side of which a main building will be erected at a later date. Constructed of tarred half-timbering° resting on ground° plates. The in-filling which is whitewashed is of bricks°.

To the south is the barn which has two rows of uprights tied together by two sets of cross beams. There is a lean-to° on both sides. On the north side the lean-to° is a little higher and wider and there is a gateway in both gable ends. This was to enable laden carts to be driven through during harvest.

A dendrochronological° dating suggests that the main part of the barn was built 1650–60. The east wing which contains stables, pigsties and rooms for farm-hands is built of timber felled 1755/56 but later additions have been made to both ends of the building. The side-wings are from a later period, the sheep-house in north-east being from 1848. The west wing is a reconstruction of the old cowshed as it was till the end of the 19th century.

Portable cowman's hut

Roller

29. FISHERMEN'S HUT FROM NYMINDEGAB, WEST JUTLAND

Huts of this type were placed together in groups of four and belonged to the joint owners of a fishing boat. One of the huts is original but to give an impression of the whole community three have been copied from old surveys and photographs; one of the four was used for storing tools and equipment.

The original hut, formerly situated in the sand dunes by the North Sea is simply a roof span thatched with reeds and lyme-grass and set on the ground. By the gable, to the left of the door there is a chimney made of sandy turf. The food was prepared on an iron trivet over the hearth. Against the back gable are two primitive bedsteads the one for the fishermen and the other for the women. Inside, also, is the figure-head of a ship; many ships were stranded on this coast.

In Nymindegab and other fishing places there were many huts of this type. The fishing boats were owned by groups of people from the inland. In spring, when the season started, the owners of a boat moved down to the coast. Each house was occupied by two couples. While the men were away fishing, the women would do the housework and dig lug-worms for bait. In the middle ages it was unusual for fishing to be a full time occupation and the tradition of using these seasonal huts can be traced back to then.

Long line

Food box

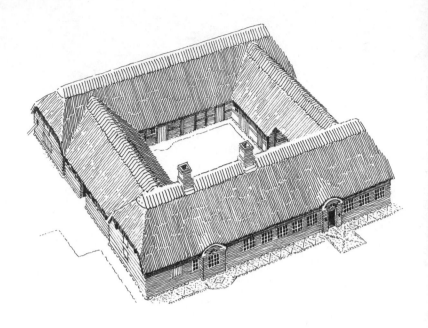

30. FARMSTEAD FROM LØNNESTAK,
WESTERN JUTLAND

Fly trap

Thatching hook

Four red brick wings built together in a rectangle, the farmstead was built 1803. There are two symmetrical projecting bays, each with a crescent dormer on the outer façade of the dwelling house. Remnants of half-timbering may be seen in the walls of the outbuildings. This was gradually replaced by brick walls during the 19th century.

The dwelling house entrance is reached by a cobbled pavement of beach stones arranged in a pattern; a wheel ornament adorns the front door. The lobby, which has a wooden barrel vault, leads into the best room furnished with chests and cupboards. Behind is a guest room with a bed and a sea chest. At the other side of the lobby is another best room, decorated with paintings from the 1870s; on the plastered walls are stencil painted patterns, and the woodwork is decorated with painted flowers. The room is heated by an iron stove fired through the wall, and the wall behind the stove has Dutch tiles arranged symmetrically. The furniture consists of an English grandfather clock, a bureau, a chest of drawers, an armchair and, below the windows, a long table in front of benches fixed to the walls and joined at the corners. There are chairs on the near side of the table. There is also a hanging paraffin lamp and on the walls a picture of a ship, family portraits etc. One door opens to a small pantry used for storing plates, cups, etc. not in everyday use, and another to a dark bedroom. Next to the second best room is the family living room, with two alcove beds with sliding doors in the wall, and by the window a table with fixed benches, at which the family had their meals in the winter. There is also a hanging paraffin lamp, American wall clock, and a shelf with a supply of medicine, bible, hymn books etc. Standing by the tiled wall is an iron stove stoked from the open chimney in the kitchen next door. Carved into the chimney are the initials of the owner, CTS, and the year 1803. Next to the kitchen chimney is a back-kitchen with a door to the salt room and an outer door to the courtyard. In the scullery, which is reached through the kitchen, there is a large open chimney with a bread oven and a fixed copper, and the family took their meals in the summer at the table by the window. Next to the chimney is the bread room, and on the other side a larger and a small bed-chamber for the farmhand. Behind the chimney the bread oven protrudes through the wall into a room in the gable used for storing hay. From here it is possible to look into part of the loft, which was used for the storage of threshed corn and utensils.

Ridge turf lifting board

From the scullery a door leads directly into the cowshed. To the left standings for five cows, to the right stalls for calves, a pigsty and a brick water trough supplied by a wooden pipe from the sweep well in the courtyard. In the cobbled floor which has a brick or timber edge there is a plank for wheeling the dung-barrow on. The dung-hill is not in the courtyard as was the practice in other parts of the country, but on the outside of the building. Beyond the cowshed under the same wing is the stable with four horse boxes, two pigsties, and in the corner above them a hencoop. Beyond the open wall of the stable is a small room with a chaff-cutter. Then follows the threshing-floor and two barns, one for rye and one for barley; the corn came in through the door or through shutters in the outer walls. A small privy in the corner is entered from the courtyard. The coachhouse also serves as the farmer's workshop; it contains a workbench and sundry tools, and the ceiling is of loose boards and sticks covered with turf. Finally there is a peat house and the covered gateway.

Peat spade

Nose-bag

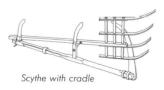

Scythe with cradle

Drag rake

31. FARMSTEAD FROM EIDERSTEDT, SOUTHWEST SCHLESWIG

This building originates from low-lying marshland protected from the sea by sluices and dykes. It is situated on an artificial mound surrounded by drainage dykes to avoid the danger of flooding. The building is almost square and is covered with a high-pitched straw roof making room for a barn in the middle which is 44 feet high to the roof ridge°. Around the barn are the living quarters on the east, the threshing floor on the south, the stable for horses and young cattle on the west and the cowsheds on the north. All these premises are in the form of wide outshots° or aisles of the main frame. This concentrated form of construction began in North Holland and East Friesland about 1600, partly because rising corn prices and increasing corn exports necessitated larger barns. The type later spread to the east and became common in the low-lying Eiderstedt peninsular. This peninsular is a part of North Friesland which was a Danish pos-

Scythe° and gathering stick

Brazier°

Restraining° yoke for sheep

session until 1864. The date of the present building is 1653 and this date together with the owner's initials A.A.H. may be seen on the southern gable. The walls are built of red bricks° which on the east and north of the dwelling quarters are larger and older than the remainder.

Feed° rack

The double doors on the west side give on to the threshing floor and there is a small entrance door on the south side in the gable end of the living quarters. An inner door connects the threshing floor with the flag stone passage. This passage contains two large wardrobes and a chest which is on wheels so that it can easily be moved out in case of fire. In the west wall are cupboard beds with shutters for the farmhands. In front of the alcove° beds is a locker which they used as seat and in front of this the long table. Over the alcoves° is a shelf for plates and dishes. On the east side of the passage, doors open into the two main rooms both with soft wood floors. The southern one with whitewashed walls is the "best° room" kept for festivities. Of note among the furniture are two carved oak cupboards, the one on the north wall typically Dutch, and a chair which could be folded to form a small table. The room has no fire-place but there is a brazier°.

Gingerbread° mould

The other door from the passage leads to the dwelling-room°, the walls of which are decorated with white and blue Frisian tiles°. To the right of the iron stove°, heated from the kitchen, is an alcove° bed with gaily painted doors and baroque carvings. On the opposite wall is a desk and a hanging cupboard with glass doors. On the wall next to the door is a Frisian hanging clock.

Thatcher's needle

Through the rear wall of the passage a door under the antlers leads to a room which is used as a scullery° with an outer door to the north. In here is an alcove° bed for the maidservant and sundry kitchen and scullery° equipment such as cheese° and butter° moulds. The east door leads to the kitchen which has a flag stone floor and a large raised open fireplace surrounded by lead-glazed green and yellow tiles°. The hearth has draught holes let into it and beneath it is a small bread° oven. When using the oven it was necessary to stand in a hole in the floor in front of it (covered with a wooden lid). There are also plate racks, a table which can be folded up against the wall and, by the window, a flat stone sink. In the north wall of the kitchen steps lead down to the vaulted cellar and also up to the larder above the cellar.

Button° mould

Butter° mould

Cheese° mould

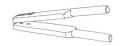

Tallow° squeezer

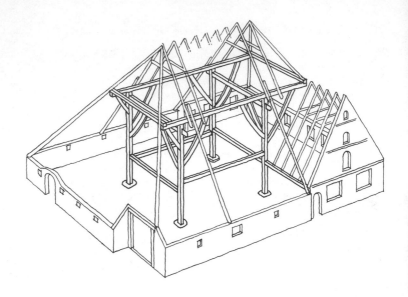

Sheep° restrainer

From the scullery° a door leads to the cowshed which has a brick° floor. From the cowshed further to the west is the stable where the horses and young cattle were stalled. To the south is the big threshing floor where the corn was threshed and where waggons, ploughs etc. now stand. A long pole used for jumping across the many dykes and ditches in the fields leans near the outer door. At harvest time the loads of corn were driven into the threshing floor from which the corn could be stacked in the barn in the middle of the building.

The characteristic building construction is best seen from the threshing floor. An exceptionally tall and heavy oak post stands in each of the four corners of the barn; they carry between them a heavy horizontal timber-frame from which the main rafters run up to the ridge°. To the east this frame protrudes a long way out in order to cover the broader living quarters. From the frame also other rafters extend downwards to the outer walls, so that the outer parts of the building can be compared with a broad lean-to. – There is no well. The cattle were watered in the channels and ditches, and water for household use was fetched from a small water hole. – In the field, north of the dykes, is a scratching post for cattle.

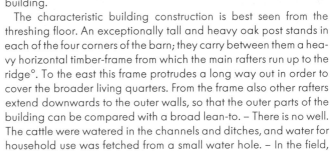

Rape° fork

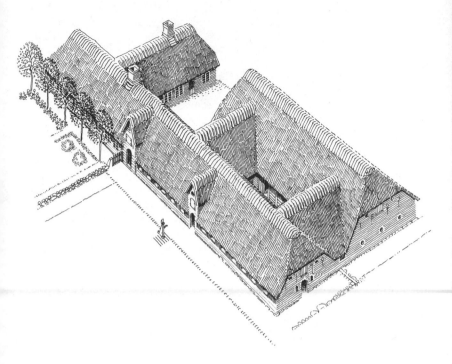

32. FARMSTEAD FROM SØNDER SEJERSLEV, NORTH SCHLESWIG

One very long wing contains the dwelling in one end and cowshed in the other. Parallel to the cowshed is the barn which is connected with the cowshed by two short cross-wings, thus forming a small courtyard. There is one more cross-wing at the dwelling-house end. The walls are mainly of red brick° but the walls of the barn are partly timbered with horizontal oak° boards laid between upright posts. Parts of the farmstead probably date back to the 17th cent. but it was extended to the present shape through extensions and rebuilding;

Well grappling iron

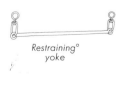

Restraining° yoke

Fodder box

Branding iron

Restrainer° for calves

Iron cooking
pot

Waffling iron

Cake mould

Coffee grinder

Flowerpot

some of these are indicated by the dates 1779 and 1823 on the iron-ties of the gables. Part of the dwelling-house was modernized in 1874, and the present state and furnishings relate to the years just after this modernization.

A narrow divided passage across the long wing separates the dwelling and the cowshed and gives a shortcut from one side of the steading to the other. The entrance to the dwelling-house is from the larger courtyard, which is open on one side, through a door in the cross-wing.

Here is the scullery° with an open° chimney. Around this room are the maidservant's bedchamber, a larder with a sunk floor, a servant's hall, where the farmer and farm-hands took their meals, and a mangling-room. From the scullery pass into the kitchen where the cooking took place on an iron range beside a closed chimney. The wall behind the range is covered with Dutch tiles. The wife and maid servants took their meals at the table in the kitchen. In the corner of this room there is a small larder.

From the kitchen into the dwelling-room° which is heated by a stove of cast iron and hollow white-glazed tiles. The wood-work of this room is partly painted in brown to resemble the grain of wood. The outside wall is covered with white and blue tiles° decorated with landscapes. The furniture comprises a bureau, table and chairs, corner-cupboard, tobacco-table, and beside the alcove° bed is a cradle. The grandfather clock, from the first half of the 18th cent. was made by the farmer at that time who worked as a clock-maker as well. From here into a small room with alcove° beds. The outside wall is covered with white and blue tiles°. A painting from 1854 shows the church and inn which could be seen through the windows. On the shelves of the bureau are silver spoons and punch-cups. On the window sill a brass sun dial from 1724, made by the same clockmaker as the grandfather clock. At the end of the dwelling-house is a best° room. The outside walls are covered with white undecorated tiles°. The unheated room was mainly used for storage purposes as can be seen from the furniture which consists of painted cupboards and chests. Connecting with this room are two small chambers.

Steel-yard

Potato° grater

Cartridge bag

Return to the dwelling-room. Between this room and the passage is the parlour, a finer sitting-room, which was arranged after the re-building of 1874. It is heated by the same stove as the dwelling-room. The walls are papered except the outside wall which is co-vered with tiles° decorated with manganese coloured flower pots. The furniture is veneered and upholstered.

In the corner of the cowshed is a closet just by the door from the passage. In this end of the cowshed there is horse stabling on one side and stalls for young cattle on the other. In the rest of the cowshed there are stalls for cows and bullocks. The numerous ex-tensions of the cowshed were due to the importance of bullock breeding in the region; an extra cowshed has been built in the end of the barn. It is entered through the cross-wing next to the dwelling-house. In this cross-wing is a servant's room with accommodation for three farm hands. From the barn low double doors lead out into the small courtyard which was formed by the extension of the cowshed. In the corner of the barn, beside the high double doors it is possible to see through into the cart-shed with sundry tools in the corner. In the barn the construction of the heavy inner uprights of the nave° and side aisle can be seen. In it are a farm wagon and agricultural implements, among which are drag-rakes, roller, harrow and wheel plough. In the cross-wing at the gable of the cowshed is a room used for such purposes as keeping calves and sheep.

Through the door in the gable, the manure was taken on a dung barrow from the cowshed to the dunghill. A little farther away is a watering-hole. Outside the front of the cowshed is a well, from which the water was pumped through a pipe into the water trough in the cowshed. Household water was pumped up from the well in the courtyard by the door from the scullery. Outside the dwelling-house is a garden which at the farther end is extended into a bleachgreen where new linen was spread on the grass to be bleached by the sun and weather.

Wall candle holder

Ink stand

Match holder

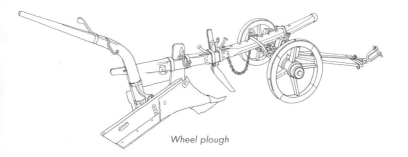

Wheel plough

33. LACE SCHOOL FROM NØRRE SEJERSLEV, NORTH SCHLESWIG

Glass bulb with water

A "longhouse"° built of red brick° with two dwellings and a cowshed. The entrance to the main dwelling is in the middle of the northern side. The dwelling of the retired occupier is entered through the gable.

Through the lobby in the middle of the house into the kitchen, which has an open° chimney with a brick hearth, in which is a bread° oven. Round the window corner there are a table and benches°.

Behind the kitchen is a lace-making room where, during part of the 19th century, the housewife taught lace-making to young girls. Each had a lace pillow and sat facing the windows to use the light. In the evening they used a glass bulb filled with water in order to concentrate the light from a candle. – Lace-making was formerly an important handicraft in the districts around Tønder in western Schleswig, especially as a domestic industry in humble homes.

Beside the kitchen is the living-room with alcove° beds, table and chairs, and a chest-of-drawers. The next room is a "best° room" only used for storage purposes. On the other side of the lobby, and entered through a separate door at the front, there is a small cowshed for a cow and a pig.

The gable-door leads through a narrow lobby into another small kitchen with an open° chimney. Here is the entrance to the living-room of the retired occupier of the house. The room is heated by an iron stove° and contains an alcove° bed, table and chairs, and a bureau.

Lace pillow   *Lace pillow for children*

34. SKIPPER'S FARMSTEAD FROM RØMØ,
NORTH SEA COAST

The small island of Rømø on the North Sea coast is sandy and infer-
tile, and the inhabitants were seamen. Most of the farmers, who
were freeholders, owned shares in a ship or sailed ships for Danish,
Dutch or other companies. In their absence the women looked after
the farms. Their ships were generally engaged in whaling off Greenland. This house is influenced by Dutch and Frisian culture. The roof
is thatched and the ridge° covered with turf. The ground plan is
T-shaped, the barn (1793) and the stable and cowshed (1773) forming the west wing.

   The main entrance is from the south between two carved stone
posts with religious inscriptions. On the left-hand post is a relief of
the man who built the house with his wife and son, dated 1767. On
the right is a relief of Christ. The posts of the garden fence are made

Nesting box
made from
a buoy

Wool-carder's basket

Bucket yoke

Sheep° restrainer

of whale ribs because of the scarcity of trees on Rømø. In front of the arched front door is the sweep well°.

Wooden
ice shoes

The dwelling-house was built about 1750 though the east gable was rebuilt in 1862. It contains several rooms with soft wood floors, alcove° beds and cupboards or lockers in the walls which are decorated like the ceiling with oil paintings. Some of the walls are covered with Dutch tiles°. The nautical instruments and ornaments brought from abroad show the occupant to have been a seafarer.

A flag stone passage divides the dwelling-part from the stable. The door to the right opens into a small bed-chamber for a servant. Then follows the winter living-room with south windows. The iron stove°, dated 1772, is stoked from the kitchen. In the glass-fronted wall cabinet is earthenware brought home from England. The grandfather clock is dated 1750 and near to it hangs a compass. The husband and wife's bed is along a passage. The next room is a "best° room". To the north lies a small room for a ship's crew with a sea-chest and a sailors barrel for salted meat. Another door leads to the loft and the cellar. To the east is another "best° room" called the "dead body room" because any member of the family who died was laid here before the funeral. The furniture includes chests. Northwards a door opens to the small spare-room with a bed for guests. From the first "best° room" a door leads to the north or summer living-room. The iron stove° is dated 1736. In the plate rack are Dutch and English earthenware, and among other things in the room are an ostrich egg and a saw from a saw-fish. The next room is the kitchen and on the raised open fireplace the openings of the stoves° can be seen. The pottery is black Jutland° made without a wheel. In the corner by the pantry hangs a rack for wooden plates. In the flagged passage there is a mousetrap on the chest and on the wall above hang whalers' knives in a wooden sheath. The door next to the hand-mill leads to the scullery°, which houses the bread° oven, kneading trough, etc. A locker in the wall holds heather for fuel; it is filled from the loft. In the north wall a door opens into a milk room.

From the scullery° and the passage there are doors to the cowshed and stable. Then follows the threshing-floor and lastly the barn.

Dish cover

Heddle° loom

Winnowing-fan

Sugar° cutters

Sickle°

37–40. BUILDINGS FROM NORTH-EASTERN SCHLESWIG

37. FUEL SHED FROM SODE

Quite a small house of horizontal oak° boards containing a room used for fuel. The top gables protrude and are supported by brackets. Over the door is carved the number 97, the meaning of which is not known.

38. BARN FROM ØSBY

A long building with horizontal oak° boards and cross braces between the tie° beams and uprights. Originally, it was divided into alternate grain stores and threshing floors. The year 1734 carved over a door does not indicate the year it was built as dendrochronological° dating suggests it is a good hundred years older.

39. BARN FROM GRØNNINGHOVED

A long building with horizontal oak° boards and cross braces between the tie° beams and uprights except over the original threshing floor where there is no tie beam in order to make room for swinging the flail°. In its place, a curved cross brace connects the upright with the rafter. Over a door is the year 1605 and the undecipherable inscription SIELIRVER.

Sledge for seaweed for the ridge

40. DWELLING-HOUSE FROM BARSØ

A longhouse° with brick walls at one end and horizontal oak° boards at the other. The brick part of the house contains the dwelling and the wooden part the stables.

Framed memorial

By the entrance from the garden, iron wall ties are dated 1766. The dwelling house was originally half-timbered° but was rebuilt in brick° by this date at the latest. A narrow lobby leads through the house from the main entrance to the back door into the courtyard. The lobby separates the scullery and stables on the one side from the dwelling rooms on the other.

Next to the lobby is the kitchen with a fireplace for cooking and an open° chimney. Nearer the courtyard is a projection with table and bench°. Adjoining this is a pantry through which there is a way down to the cellar°. Next to the pantry is a narrow passage to a maid's room. The door at the side of the fireplace leads to the dwelling room°.

This is heated by an iron stove° stoked from the kitchen. On the plate rack under the ceiling are pewter plates (replicas). To one side are two alcove° beds. The alcove door on the extreme right retains a layer of paint which is earlier than the red on the walls. The door between the alcove beds leads to an unheated room. On the tie° beams there is painted decoration of stylized vines which is older than the other painting in the room and, in fact, goes back to the period when the whole house was wooden. The next room is a best° room, painted blue with marbling on the alcove doors and ceiling. On the tie beams at the end there are remnants of earlier decoration. This unheated room was used mainly for storage and the furniture was made for that purpose.

Besom

On the other side of the lobby is a scullery° with an open° chimney and a bread° oven. From here a door leads to the farm servant's room in the wooden part of the house adjoining the stable, threshing floor and cowshed. This portion of the house had been demolished before the museum acquired it and has been reconstructed on the basis of an early survey and some photographs.

41. SHOEMAKER'S COTTAGE FROM ØDIS
BRAMDRUP, NEAR KOLDING, EASTERN JUTLAND

A longhouse° with the dwelling part at the south end and the stall at the north. It is built of heavy half-timbering° which was previously used in an earlier building. The bays at the southern end rest on ground°plates; the southern and northern end appear to be more recent than the middle. Where there is no ground° plate the uprights rest on small piles of stones which were placed there when the bottom of the uprights rotted. The in-filling is of brick° but many of the uprights have grooves indicating that at a previous date there were boards between them.

Heeltool

In the middle of the building facing the road there is an entrance which leads into the kitchen. Here as in the other parts of the building there are cross braces between the beams and the uprights. There is an open° chimney with a brick° fireplace and a fire hole for stoking the bake oven and another for the stove° in the dwelling-room°. In the dwelling-room° there are alcove° beds in the wall opposite the windows and a bed in a small room in the corner by the door which leads to the "best° room".

Returning to the kitchen another door leads to the workshop° for shoemaking. Over the outside door to the stalls is a carving table from another building which bears the date 1733.

Shoemaker's hammer

Pincers

Last

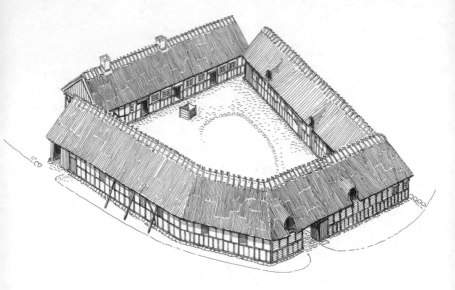

42. FARMSTEAD FROM TRUE, EASTERN JUTLAND

This steading comes from the eastern part of Jutland which has a rather fertile soil and a milder climate than the west coast. The farmers are traditionally well-to-do and industrious people.

The half-timbering° of the walls is painted black while the infilling, which is partly wattle° and daub and partly sun-dried° and real bricks°, is painted red. The ridge of the thatched roof is held down by roof-trees°. The four wings are built together round the courtyard, but the ground plan is not a rectangle because of the shape of the old village road.

The covered gateway through the western wing (where a wagon stands the wheels of which are secured with lynch° pins) leads into the cobbled courtyard, which contains the midden (the uncobbled area where manure is heaped) and a well. To the north is the dwelling-house. At the west end a door opens into a small cobbled entry.

Wooden
steel-yard

Candle mould

Flax° carder

Candle drying frame

From here to the left a door leads into the scullery°, where the baking and brewing were done. In here is a sunk open fireplace with a bread° oven at the rear and a fixed° copper (a large copper pot set in bricks° and clay and used to boil water for making beer) which is stoked from the fire-place. Over the chimney hang some sausage-fillers and an oven° peel, a long spade-like instrument used to place bread in the oven. To the left are implements for baking, brewing, candle° making, etc. The bench, used for slaughtering animals, is made out of an old bier from a church. A door opens into the garden, which represents the period about 1875.

Pepper° grinder

From the entry the door to the right leads into the kitchen-sitting room, which was for everyday use. Note the date, 1759, over the fireplace. A long table and benches stand by the windows and there is a large wooden beer mug on the table. All the members of the household drank from this mug. Over the master's seat at the end of the table is a locker and a shelf for pewter plates. A door opens into the maidservant's primitive bedroom under the staircase. Next to it is a door to the larder in which most of the earthenware comes from Sorring (see no. 43). Across a further cobbled entry is the parlour containing an iron stove° with rococo ornaments. To the north there were once alcove° beds, but about 1850 they were replaced by a bedroom and a larder. At the east gable end is the "best° room" which could not be heated and was used only for festive occasions; its normal daily use was for the storage of textiles and textile implements. It contains a four-poster bed for guests, a press and chests. A door opens into the courtyard.

Tankard

In the eastern wing are the cowsheds, the servant's room and the farmer's workshop°. In the west wing there are barns and threshing floors, one for each type of corn. In the south-west corner a part of the dividing wall is left unfinished to show the upright laths on which the clay is thrown. Nearby is a tool for twisting straw° rope.

Dough scraper

In the south wing is the stable and the covered gateway leading to no. 43.

Copper° lustre cream jug

Mustard mill

Wheel with lynch° pin

Braiding loom

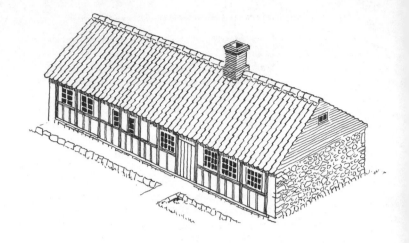

43. POTTER'S WORKSHOP FROM SORRING, EASTERN JUTLAND

Slip-horn°

The country around the village of Sorring was at one time a centre of Danish lead-glazed pottery manufacture. The pottery was made by the peasants as an extra source of income.

The workshop was built in 1844. The door on the eastern side leads to the potter's kiln, which is made of sun-dried° bricks, although the bricks have become partially fire-baked through use. In the chimney, on the west wall, is the oven used to melt the lead, the top of the molten lead being skimmed off and used in the making of the glaze. To the left, in the chimney, is the arched kiln in which the pottery was baked. It is divided from the chimney by a wall pierced with holes to allow draught in which there is also an opening for entering the kiln and stacking the pottery. During the firing this opening is closed with bricks. On the opposite wall of the kiln are three holes for firing; these are closed with large clay bowls.

The door to the north leads from the passage-way to the potter's workroom. Here under the window is a low table for working the clay. In the corner by the door are two potter's wheels for shaping

Clay° knife

Flint-mill   *Pug° mill*   *Potter's wheel*

the pottery. The potter is seated while he works. The clay is placed on the upper wheel and the lower wheel is turned with the foot. There is a long brick° stove to produce heat for drying the unfired pots which were stored in the roof. Before firing the pots were covered with slip clay to give an even surface (or if a white finish was desired with slip pipe clay). Decoration could be applied with a slip-horn° or patterns could be scratched on the clay. Finally the pots were glazed and fired. In days gone by a dry powder consisting of lead ash and diatomaceous peat from a neighbouring moor was sifted on, but about 1880 the potters of Sorring began using a liquid glaze of red lead, powdered flint and flour paste.

Twig° for decorating pots

Stilt

Scraper

Dog mould

Rosette stamp

Handle press

Cutting wire

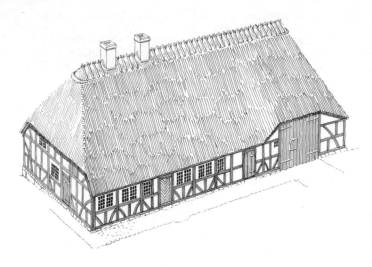

44–45. BUILDINGS FROM THE ISLAND OF ALS

44. SMALLHOLDER'S FARMSTEAD FROM DYNDVED

A longhouse° but rather broad, with a bay projecting at the side towards the garden. The walls are half-timbered° with a lot of short braces and the in-filling is of small bricks°. To the right of the lobby is the kitchen with an open° chimney. From here a door leads to the living-room with two alcove° beds, over which the initials of the owner and his wife. He was a seaman who had gone ashore and married in 1800, at which time the house seems to have been rebuilt. Although the house is older, the furniture is partly somewhat younger.

Behind the living-room is a best° room with indoor shutters for the windows. Here are chests and textile implements. From the kitchen there is a passage to the small stable with room for one horse and one or two cows. At the end of the house there is a threshing floor inside a gateway and a barn and pigsty.

At the other end of the house, to the left of the main entrance, is the dwelling of the retired occupiers of the house. The kitchen has an open° chimney with a small bread° oven. The living-room is heated by an iron stove° and has two alcove° beds.

Hackle holder

Ember scoop

45. WOODEN BARN FROM STEVNING

The barn is a six-bay stack shed with a passage for carts through the two central bays. Originally it was a detached building and as such it is re-erected although for a long time it was built together with other outbuildings of a farmstead.

The barn has a heavy framework with many braces. According to dendrochronology° the oaktrees for the timber were felled in 1744. On the outside the construction is covered by vertical boards except the wall° plate and uprights which stand directly on the ground° sill.

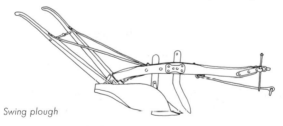

Swing plough

The buildings nos. 54–59 come from the former Danish regions of South Sweden, the provinces of Scania and Halland which were given up to Sweden in 1658, and from the province of Småland. In southwestern Scania most buildings were half-timbered°. The native Danish forest trees being foliate, old buildings in the wooded districts were built of oak°. The ends of the horizontal boards are mortised into the dividing upright posts; the roofs are thatched. Further north, the Danish boundary included areas of fir forest and timber from coniferous trees was used for house construction, the walls built of horizontal logs°.

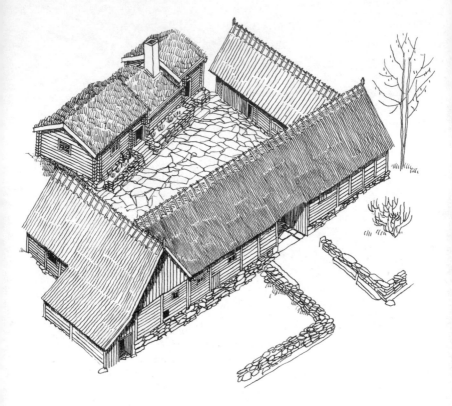

54. FARMSTEAD FROM HALLAND, SWEDEN

Flax° distaff°

The dwelling-house is north of the paved courtyard. In front of it is a strip of garden supported by a dry stone wall. The house is built of heavy horizontal fir logs° with corner joints. The lower house in the middle, which has no ceiling, originates from the latter half of the 17th century while the two houses on either side were added later and have ceilings, being descendants of the loft house (see no. 57). The roof is turf covered and between the turf and the boards which support it is a layer of birch bark to keep out the moisture. The stone steps near the straw hives lead into a narrow passage. To the left a

Coffee grinder

Wooden box

Cheese° mould

door opens into the "distaff° room", where the weaving and other textile work was done. To the right is the kitchen-living room. The sloping roof boards are supported by a ridge° beam and two side beams which rest upon the gables. The only window is in the roof and the position of this derives from the "louver"° or smoke hole which was similarly situated in the days when an open hearth was used at floor level. At a later date a raised open fireplace with a coved mantle was added for cooking, heating and lighting; behind it is a bread° oven. In front of the fireplace is a table at which the occupants took their meals. Along the northern and western walls are fixed benches° covered with homespun material. In front of the bench by the dividing wall is the long table, which was used for festivals. A cabinet for the farmer's papers and a grandfather clock stand on the bench. In the south wall are two alcove° beds for the family with a locker between them. Near the dresser on the eastern dividing wall, a door opens into the pantry where some of the household work was done.

Pine light holder

In the days when light came only from the smoke hole in the roof it was a peasant custom to put the table and the long bench° by the dividing wall. When, however, the chimney was introduced and glass windows in the walls replaced the smoke hole, the long table and the benches were moved to the window corner. This can be seen in the other buildings, e.g. nos. 1, 8, 42, 63 and 71. The introduction of the chimney also made it possible to have a ceiling.

The three wings containing farm buildings are constructed at right angles and enclose three sides of the courtyard. The walls are timbered with heavy horizontal boards laid between upright posts (see no. 55). The thatched roof is supported by ridge° beams running lengthwise through the buildings and supported on ridge° posts or high upright posts (see no. 71). In the buildings to the west of the covered gateway are a barn, cowsheds, pigsties, stable and sheep shed. Note here the high ridge-posts which are situated in the dividing wall. To the east lie a barn and threshing floor which have wooden floors, and sliding shutters instead of doors. In the east wing is the workshop°. – East from the farm is a **roadside stone** from Halland (see no. 60).

Hand harrow for slashing and burning

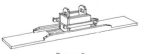

Potato° grater

Flax° braker

Juniper° mill

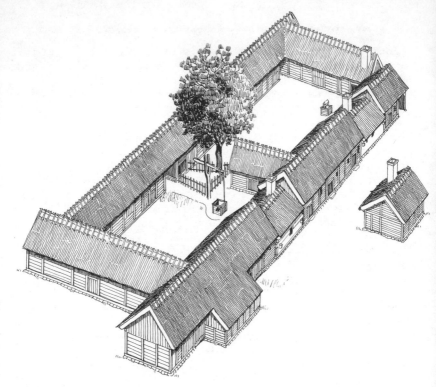

55. TWIN FARMSTEAD FROM GÖINGE,
SCANIA, SWEDEN

Butter churn°

This type of farm, built for two neighbouring owner-occupiers, each of whom occupied one half of the rectangular steading, was known as a "twin-house". A cross-wing and a gate divide the two court-yards. The walls are built of heavy horizontal oak° boards between upright posts; the roofs are thatched. Most of the buildings date from the 18th century, but the lower whitewashed portions of the south wing of this steading are, in fact, older.

The eastern steading is approached through the covered gateway. To the south is the dwelling-house. Near the gateway and the winch

*Pack carrier
for horses*

Hanger for pig carcase

Wooden pot

Mustard° grinder

well° is a room in which the hand-loom is kept. Over the door a cross and the date 1737 are carved. Further west another door leads into a cobbled passage. Part of the dividing wall here was originally in a late medieval house. In the chamber to the right are chests and a bed. In the kitchen-living room to the left is a raised open fireplace with a bread° oven behind it, and an iron stove°. A small fire could be made in the niche in the corner of the chimney breast to light the room. In front of the bench° attached to the dividing wall is the long table (see no. 54). On the wall hang paintings of biblical scenes, characteristic of local peasant art about 1800. The eastern wing approached from the courtyard contains several rooms, including the scullery. In the north wing are barns, stables and cowsheds. The gate to the west leads into the courtyard of:

Baby° walker

The western steading which contains a sweep well°. In the north wing are the workshop° and the cowsheds. The west wing contains a barn. The dwelling house lies to the south. On the northeast cornerpost of the whitewashed wall are carved a cross and the date 1688, this is the oldest part.

Inside the dwelling house are several small rooms and the kitchen-living room, which contains a raised open fireplace with an arched opening and a bread° oven in a corner at the back. The room has no ceiling. The sloping planked roof was formerly covered with turf and was later thatched. There is a heavy ridge° beam and two side beams which rest on the gables. In front of the walls are benches° the tops of which are stuffed with straw and covered with homespun material to form beds. The children or maidservants slept there, while the husband and wife slept in the bed along the back wall. The long table is laid as it would be for a Christmas dinner. The cross beam in front of the table indicates the "part of distinction" of the room, while the cross beam by the fireplace indicates the kitchen part. A stranger entering, possibly a beggar, had to wait for the farmer's permission before he passed this "beggar beam". Under the covered gateway at the western end of the dwelling an old type of roof construction can be seen – cross-laid sticks and juniper laths tied together with lime bast. The small building outside to the south is a scullery°.

Oven° peel and oven scraper

Cake° spit

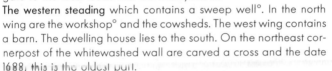

Flax° scutcher

Pine° light holder

56. KILN FROM SMÅLAND, SWEDEN

A small house for drying grain, malt, flax etc. The walls are built of horizontal fir logs° with corner joints; the roof is of turf. The western gable forms shelter in front of the door which was used for braking flax° or for domestic work. Inside the building are broad shelves on which the grain or flax° etc. was placed for drying. In the corner to the left of the door is the stove. It has no chimney and is constructed of lumps of granite. The smoke found its way out through the door and the openings in the wall. The steam baths which were formerly used in Scandinavian countries were built in the same manner. Steam for the bath was produced by pouring water on the hot surface of the stove. – Kilns of different types are found on the east side of the Baltic, in Sweden and the Faeroes. Foundations of a house similar to number 56 have been found in a medieval Icelandic settlement in Greenland.

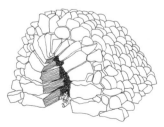

Kiln stove

57. LOFT HOUSE FROM SOUTH-EASTERN ŚMALAND, SWEDEN

The two-storied building was once part of a farm and was used as a storehouse. It is built of fir baulks which are interlocked at the corners. The roof is turf. In front of the upper storey is a balcony with an outside ladder. In the ground floor rooms are a number of utensils including a large flour bin, a salt trough, barrels for whortleberries and butter, vats for brewing juniper water, implements for baking and slaughtering and racks for hanging salted meat. The loft was used for storing corn, and often in summer time as a sleeping place for young people and guests.

From old manuscript sources it is clear that there were once loft houses in Denmark but they went out of use at the time that ceilings were introduced because as a result the dwelling house had a loft (see no. 54).

Similar buildings, constructed for defence in times of trouble, are known to have existed on the great medieval farms in Scandinavia. According to popular folk songs, such buildings were also used as ladies' bowers.

Dough kneader

Wooden bin

Rack for salted meat

Potato° grater

Cheese° mould and drainer

58. WATER MILL FROM WESTERN SMÅLAND, SWEDEN

Simple water mills with rather primitive horizontal wheels were frequently built on small streams and used only in wet seasons when there was plenty of water. They are called "splash" mills and are no longer found in southern Scandinavia. They belonged to an individual farmer and ground corn for that farm only.

The mill house is built of horizontal fir logs° interlocked at the corners; the roof is of shingle. The horizontal wheel is situated directly under the mill stones and the whole building straddles a narrow stream. A wooden trough leads the mill race to the slanting vanes of the mill (see nos. 6 and 17).

Mechanism of the mill

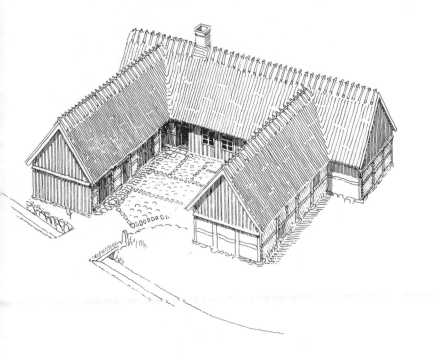

59. SMALLHOLDER'S COTTAGE FROM DÖRRÖD, SCANIA, SWEDEN

The cottage is thought to date back to the 18th century; the west wing, however, was built during the first half of the 19th century, at a time when the farmer may have bought more land. The house appears now as it was about 1880, before the death of the husband of the last inhabitant.

The three wings are constructed at right angles and enclose the courtyard which opens south to the village street. The small stream running along the street passes through a culvert under the drive to the cobbled courtyard.

The house is half-timbered° with the uprights placed directly on the stone sill. The beams are mortised into the uprights. Most of the framework is filled with wattle° and daub, and the walls are white-

Washing° bat

Grain measure

Washing bench

Beet lifter

Whisk

Cake mould

washed all over. The front of the central wing was reconstructed, however, in the last half of the 19th century, when the windows were enlarged and the wall was rebuilt with sun-dried bricks and boarded on the outside. The upright gables are boarded with the exception of the west gable of the central wing which is made of juniper wattle; in the narrow passage between the central and the west wings is an old gable which is also of juniper wattle. Constructional details such as the half-timbering and boarded gables closely resemble building practices on Zealand. This resemblance characterizes the south-western part of Scania, whereas in the north-eastern part, which is rich in forests, wooden buildings were common (cf. no. 55).

The entrance is in the front of the central wing. A small lobby leads into the dwelling-room° which is heated by an iron stove° bearing the name of King Carl XIII of Sweden (1809–18). This stove is stoked from the chimney through a hole in the wall. In front of the windows is a longbench and a table with a stone top; at the head of the table is the master's seat and on the wall above a shelf and corner cupboard. There is also a cradle, folding bed, and a bench which can also be used as a bed. A framed paper memorial, a birthday greeting, and an American clock hang on the wall. Behind is a small room containing chests, a cupboard and a loom with a half-finished rag carpet. From the lobby there is an entrance into the large open° chimney. To the right is the raised open hearth for cooking, and in the wall can be seen the hole for stoking the dwelling room stove; at the rear is the clay bread° oven which projects from the back of the house under a lean-to. Next is the pantry with a large grain bin and various household utensils, and behind that is the larder.

A low partition wall divides the barn at the end of the central wing from the threshing floor in the east wing. On the threshing floor stand a winnowing machine, a chaff-cutter, and other implements. At the gable in this wing is a stable with standings for a horse, a cow, and a heifer. At the extreme end of the west wing there is storage space for implements including a cart, and a plough. Next to this is the pigsty, henhouse, and in the farmer's workshop nearest to the central wing stands a hand grinding mill. The well is reached by the passage between the central and the west wings.

Snuffbox

Sticks for closing sausages

60. WEAVER'S COTTAGE FROM TYSTRUP, ZEALAND

A long half-timbered° cottage with uprights placed directly on the stone sill with short pieces of timber between them. Originally, the whitewashed walls were filled in with wattle° and daub but later some sections were filled in with bricks°. As the ground slopes the western wall is lower and it is built up at the bottom with bricks° and boulders. The roof is thatched. The northern end gable is made in a very old traditional way by pressing thick straw coils down between sticks. The southern gable has a lean-to° roof carried on forked uprights – a form of construction which dates from prehistoric times and is occasionally found in houses which the inhabitants have built themselves without the help of a carpenter. (See no. 73 and the shed of no. 63).

The double doors in the middle of the eastern side lead to a small kitchen which also serves as an entrance hall. Note the split, rather than sawn, boards of the ceiling which come from a much older house. In the kitchen is a raised open hearth under the chimney on which the food was cooked. At the rear of the chimney is a bread oven which protrudes on the western side of the house under a small lean-to°. The bread° oven, the iron stove° in the dwelling-room° and the fixed° copper in the scullery° were all stoked from the chimney place.

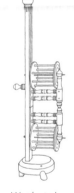

Wool winder

Wooden tub

Tinder° box

Straw° basket

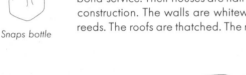

Slasher

A door to the right leads into the dwelling-room° which has a clay floor and iron stove°. In the corner of the western wall is a bed with a built-in cupboard in one end. Under the window on the same side is the long table. Along the dividing wall by the bed is a grandfather clock. Near the eastern wall stands a loom for the former owner wove for peasants who had spun their own yarn. There is also a chest° of drawers and a folding° bed for children. At the north gable there is a small room which could not be heated. In it there are, among other things, a cupboard, a chest and a bed for guests.

To the south of the kitchen is the scullery with a fixed° copper and a larder in the southwestern corner. There is also a workshop the contents of which include a shaving° horse and clogmaker's tools. In the lean-to° are two small sheds for two hens and two pigs.

Originally the house had a small outbilding to the east by the road which contained a barn and threshing floor, a bunker for fuel and standings for two cows.

Snaps bottle

Nos. 60–66 come from Zealand. The peasants of Zealand were not as free as those of Jutland and Funen and were subject to severe bond-service. Their houses are half-timbered° and mostly of slighter construction. The walls are whitewashed all over or covered with reeds. The roofs are thatched. The ridge° is fastened by roof-trees°.

Ladle

GRANITE SLABS FROM A ROAD NEAR
JÆGERSPRIS, ZEALAND

These stones were formerly placed at the side of the road to indicate the section which each farmer was responsible for keeping in repair. The farmer's initials and the number of his farm in the village were carved on the stone.

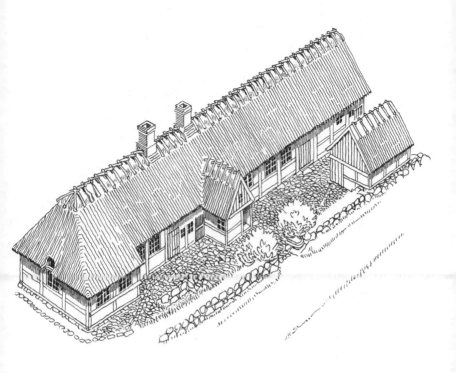

61. RURAL CRAFTSMEN'S COTTAGES FROM
KALVEHAVE, ZEALAND

A half-timbered°, thatched, long building. The walls are whitewashed all over but the west side is also in part reed covered. The
five middle bays are the oldest, built 1693–94 as a small house for a
soldier; the framework of these bays stands directly on a stone sill
with short pieces of timber between the bases of the uprights. At a
later date the building has been extended at the north and south
ends; in 1835 another room was added on to the south end and in
1869 the broader addition was made. The newest section of the
house is the northern bay. The infilling of the older walls is partly
wattle° and daub but in the extensions it is sun-dried° brick. On the
east side at the north end is a small outhouse; the infilling of the walls
is split granite and brick except at the north end where the wall is

Pit saw

*Wheelwright's°
reamer*

*Wheelwright's°
breast auger*

Plumb rule

made intirely of granite and the gable end is made of seaweed pressed in between sticks in horizontal layers.

The house, as it now stands, shows the living conditions c. 1870–80 when it was occupied by two craftsmen. At the northern end are the barn and a shed for one cow and a few pigs and sheep. The entrance is in the middle of the eastern side through the porch. To the north is the oldest part with clay floors. In the dwelling-room° there are benches° round the window corner. Following the medieval tradition the table stands in front of the partition wall (see nos. 54 and 72). In the south-western corner is a bed with a cupboard in one end. Through the door to the north is a "best° room", containing a cupboard and chest, which is unusual in that it also serves as a workshop° for the occupier. Like many woodland smallholders he was a worker in underwood, making such things as barrel hoops, wooden rakes, handles, wooden spoons, woven baskets, etc., which were taken to the local markets on a push cart. The tools of his trade are on view as well as a number of half-finished wooden articles.

To the left of the iron stove in the dwelling-room° is the door to the kitchen which also serves as a scullery°. It has a raised hearth in the chimney with a fixed° copper to the left and a bread° oven at the rear projecting under a lean-to° on the west wall. In the corner is a hand° mill and the room opposite the chimney leads to the larder.

The southern end of the house was occupied by a wheelwright°. The entrance is from the east through the small kitchen with a raised hearth into the dwelling-room°. This has a deal floor (soft wood) and an iron stove°, an expanding bed, cupboard, folding° bed and chairs. Most of the furniture was made by the wheelwright° himself. At the side of the grandfather clock on the north wall a door leads to the larder.

*Glazier's
carrying rack*

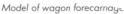

Model of wagon forecarriage

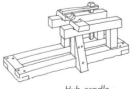

Hub cradle

The wheelwright's° shop, built in 1869, has its own outer door. It contains varios wheelwright's° tools, among them a lathe. The wheelwright° was also a carpenter, cooper and glazier. In the small outhouse to the north the wood and push cart were kept. By the stone wall in front of the house is a saw-pit over which trunks could be sawn with the pit saw that hangs under the workshop beam. One man stood on top and steered the saw while the other pulled it from below.

Clamp

Wheelwright's° plane

Felloe horse

Keg

By the road side to the west of no. 61 is a square hewn **granite milestone** from the Copenhagen – Lyngby – Hillerød main road. On one side are engraved the monogram of King Christian V (1670–1699) and the figure 1 indicating one Danish mile (four English miles) from Copenhagen. On the other side is the monogram of King Frederik V (1746–1766) and 1¼ M for 1¼ Danish miles. This later inscription dates from a more recent use of the stone. – At one time there were only few wooden mile-posts on the King's highway and these were put up at the end of the sixteenth century. When the Danish astronomer Ole Rømer (1614–1710) undertook the first systematic survey of Danish main roads, King Christian V had systematic mile-posts erected. Some of these were, however, also only wooden and situated on small artificial mounds but they were not kept in order. At the end of the eighteenth century milestones were erected all over the country.

62. FARM LABOURER'S COTTAGE FROM
ENGLERUP, ZEALAND

This belonged to a near by estate and was occupied by one of the workers. A small half-timbered° cottage with outshots°. The walls are whitewashed and partly covered with reeds. The roof is thatched. The cottage was originally poorly constructed; it had a clay floor, a much lower ceiling and the stove° and furniture were very primitive. It appears now as it was about 1900 when housing standards had improved.

At the west end a door opens into the kitchen which has a raised hearth in the chimney. Then follows the dwelling-room°, the furniture of which represents the period of the last occupier. Behind the kitchen is a small larder with an outer door opening into the garden where the small building is a pigsty. The east end of the cottage contains a small barn where, among other things, there are thatching tools and a frame for making peat. There are small boxes for sheep, a cow and a calf.

Ratchet° hanger

Wool carders

Thatcher's° bat

Peat mould

Thatcher's° comb

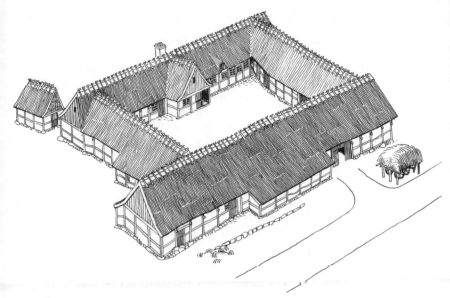

63. FARMSTEAD FROM PEBRINGE, ZEALAND

Built in rectangular form with several outshots°. Half-timbering° filled partly with wattle° and daub, partly with limestone and partly with bricks°. In its original position the walls had begun to settle on account of weak construction. In front of the south wing is the midden and a small nursery bed for kale surrounded by a wattle fence. To the right an open shed for wagons and implements is built in a traditional way; the roof is a stack of loose straw placed upon horizontal poles which rest in the Y-shaped top of the uprights. The covered gateway leads through the south wing into the cobbled courtyard. The dwelling-house is on the north side. Half-doors open into the brick-floored porch which leads into the living-room with a clay floor. The long table stands before the fixed benches° along the window wall. The smaller bench against the carved panelling from about 1625 is the farmer's seat. It was a post-renaissance

Flail

Wattle fulling board to thicken cloth

Skimming pan

Flax braker

Wooden stand

Butter churn°

Hanging candlestick

peasant custom for the sons and farm servants to sit on the long bench° under the windows while the women took their meals on the other side of the table, and either stood, or sat on seats without backs. After meals people licked their horn spoons clean and hung them up by the window. In the small hanging cabinet in the corner the farmer kept his papers and other articles of value. On the bench° below are his spirit decanter – called a "clucking bottle" and his tobacco box. Against the back wall are two beds with curtains woven at home. The iron stove° is stoked through the wall from the kitchen fire. Behind the stove, by the north window, is the cradle and below the stove is the grandmother's armchair. The door by the grandfather clock opens into a small chamber with a folding bed. Next is the "best° room" added about 1800. From the dwelling-room° a door by the stove opens into the kitchen with its large open chimney dated 1779 with a raised hearth for the fire on which trivets and pots stand. Hangers for other cooking pots are suspended from an iron bar. The mouth of the bread° oven, at the rear, is now bricked up, but the fire holes of the iron stove° and the fixed° copper can still be seen. Opposite is the larder. Next is the brick-floored scullery° with its copper. At the end there is a room for fuel and household utensils. Note the salting trough cut from one piece of wood. In a corner is a heap of white sand for strewing on the clay floors. The little room was for the maidservant to sleep in. From the scullery° two doors open into the courtyard and the garden. In the garden is a sweep well° and a pigsty. The style of the garden and the plants are of the period 1775–1800. A covered passage at the east end leads from the garden back into the courtyard. In the passage is the workshop. Over the door, inscribed in the clay of the wall, is the date of the east wing – 1798.

Also, in this wing is a sheep house. Next is a barn and threshing floor with winnowing machine, thatcher's comb and wagons, etc. In the south wing, west of the covered gateway, is a cowshed and stable. In the west range are poultry houses etc.

Hanging candlestick

Rope° hook for wagon

Sieve° holder

Food box

Words marked with a ring° can be found in the Glossary on page 82

The house belonged to a large estate, the occupant being a tenant°. The present building dates from about 1800 but some parts are older, for example, the bays, where the main cross beams are mortised very low into the upright posts, are 17th century. Excavations on the original site of the house have uncovered traces of habitation as much as 2000 years old. The oldest layer found was from the foundation of a hut, dating from the last centuries B.C. Then followed a house floor with an open hearth from about 1200 A.D. and, finally, another floor with remains of a primitive stove without a chimney from the 16th century (see no. 56).

Wooden fork

Shed for implements

Wooden fork

Hand° mill

Malt bin°

Cheese° press

64. POORHOUSE FROM GREVE, ZEALAND

Founded and built in 1710 by the local landowner on the income from church tithes. From that time until acquired by the museum, the building had housed the poor and homeless.

A longhouse° with seven dwellings. The yellow-washed walls are half-timbered° and set on a ground° plate; the infilling is partly wattle° and daub and partly brick° which was used during a restoration of the south wall in the nineteenth century. The roof is hipped°. Being rather more solid than typical Zealand buildings, the construction is probably influenced by institutional building methods.

The dwelling in the east end contains an exhibition about the history of the house and the system of poor relief.

Then follow the other dwellings, fitted up according to different periods. The oldest one is from the middle of the 18th century. Here is an open° chimney just inside the entrance and an iron stove° in the living-room which has a clay floor. In the next dwelling, from the 1840s, a small room is separated. There is also a dwelling from the 1890s. The two youngest dwellings, from the interwar period and the 1960s, have softwood floors. These dwellings are heated from modern stoves, one of them for fuel oil. In the kitchens at the back of the house the cookers are for kerosine and electricity respectively.

The western end of the house was the dwelling of the "reader". He was responsible for the religious exercises of the inmates of the house in the socalled room of prayer behind his living-room. His dwelling is from the 1840s. He was given the grandfather clock in order to be punctual in summoning for hours of prayer.

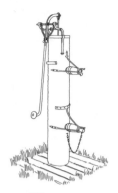

Village pump
from Pepringe,
Zealand

Boundary stone
from Virum,
Zealand

66. FIRE STATION FROM KIRKE-SÅBY, ZEALAND

Built about 1850 as a parish building to house the village fire engine.

Ridge-post construction

Buildings nos. 67–71 (and 6) come from Funen, the large fertile island between Zealand and Jutland and the native island of Hans Christian Andersen. The country people have always been relatively well-to-due; most of them were tenants°. The houses are half-timbered° with a wooden ground° sill – in fact the use of timber is almost excessive. The use of wall framing carried up above the tie° beam to act as a ridge° post in the construction of many buildings is known to date back a very long way; the rafters° of the roof rest upon a ridge° beam supported by a row of such tall ridge° posts running the length of the building. The old traditional uprights of this kind had Y-shaped top to carry the ridge° beam; later, however, they were mortised. – The walls were previously filled with wattle° and daub but in later years sun-dried° or real bricks° were used and these were whitewashed every spring. The timber was painted mainly with a reddish colour. The roofs were thatched and the ridge° fastened by roof-trees°. – Hops° were, in time gone by, a very common crop and the farmers sold them to other parts of the country. In the summer time you will see hops growing up poles or straw ropes.

Hops growing on straw ropes

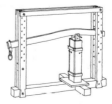

Hop° press

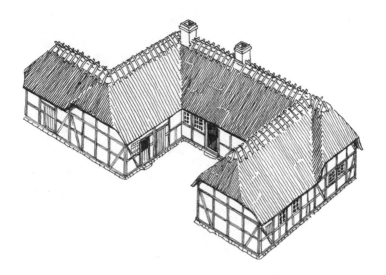

67. SMALLHOLDER'S FARMSTEAD FROM ÅRUP, FUNEN

Originally built with three wings, the eastern wing was added later. Over the front-door is an inscription beginning: "I Jesu navn er jeg opsat" ("In Jesus' name I am built") and the date 1760. A lobby leads in to the kitchen beyond with a raised open fireplace. To the right a dwelling-room° with an iron stove°; alcove° beds behind doors in the wall and a long table by the window. There is no bench because the tenant° had no farm servants. Next is an unheated "best° room" containing a chest and chest° of drawers, textile implements etc. Beyond the kitchen is the back kitchen or scullery° with a hearth, bread° oven, fixed° copper and larder.

In the western wing is a room for the previous tenant° who had re-tired from the holding. His keep was provided by the new tenant°. In the eastern wing are a cowshed and barn. To the east is the extra wing with a wooden press for putting home-grown hops° into bar-rels for sale. – The garden represents the period 1775–1800.

The occupier was a smallholder and tenant° of an estate.

Tow° distaff°

Doughnut baking pan

Bed° wagon

Watch stand

Flax° scutcher

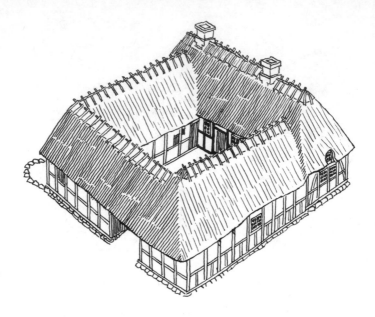

68. SMALLHOLDER'S FARMSTEAD FROM KIRKE-SØBY, FUNEN

Built in rectangular form. The occupant was a clog maker. His sign is to be seen by the covered gateway. The north wing is a barn and the east contains the threshing-floor and cowshed. Further to the south are small pens for hens and pigs. The low west wing was formerly the dwelling-house, but later became the workshop for clog-making. The south side forms the newer dwelling-house built in 1839. Through the cobbled lobby is the main living-room with raised open fireplace, chimney-crane and iron trivet, two alcove° beds and a long table by the windows. Beyond is the "best° room" containing an alcove° bed with glass panels in the doors. The entrance hall also leads into the back kitchen with bread° oven and fixed° copper alongside stoked from the open fireplace. On the south side of the cottage the bread oven projects under a lean-to°.

Dinner° pail for woman during confinement

Harvest barrel

Salt trough

Candle dip

FLAX KILN FROM ÆRØ

The kiln is built of granite and brick – granite base and brick on top.
The fire was made through the bottom opening and the flax was put
in from the top, resting on the transverse iron bars. For further parti-
culars see under flax° preparation.

69. VILLAGE MEETING PLACE

On the village° green is a pond and a village° meeting place – a
ring of stones under a lime tree. In the days of the open fields when
village° meetings were held every farmer had his own stone to sit on.
At these meetings decisions were taken about the various farming
practices; e.g. what day plowing should begin.

70. FORGE FROM ØRBÆK, FUNEN

Hoof trimmer

Built about 1845. The west gable forms a covered place for shoeing horses. The door from it leads into the smithy with its forge, bellows and tools. Next to this is the small dwelling of the smith's family. The brick-floored entrance serves as a back kitchen with a raised open fireplace and bread° oven. In the living-room is an iron cooking stove for use during the winter and an alcove° bed. Beyond is a chamber with a fourposter° bed and a folding° bed for children. Under the eastern gable is a lean-to° for fuel and a pig.

Grid-iron

Fleam° and fleamstick

Fish plate with fixed mustard pot

Sugar° cutters

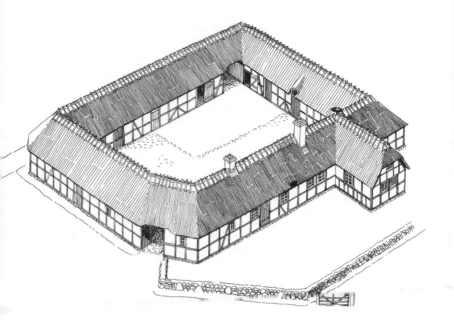

71. FARMSTEAD FROM LUNDAGER, FUNEN

The dwelling-house and range of buildings containing stables, cowshed, barns etc. is built in rectangular form enclosing a cobbled courtyard. The short side-wing was a later addition and projects from the south side towards the garden. The half-timbering° is painted reddish brown and the infilling is whitewashed. The roof which is constructed with ridge° posts is thatched.

Entering by the covered gateway the dwelling-house is across the courtyard to the south; over the front door is the date 1747. Inside the lobby a door to the left opens into a "best° room", which cannot be heated and was used only for parties or festivals. Normally it was used for storing textile implements, etc. Expanding bed for guests.

Mangle° board

Taper° holder

Washing° bat

Tobacco cutter

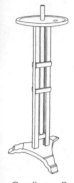

Candlestand°

Bacon° rack

Pepper° grinder

Beyond this is the side wing, in which is another "best° room" with chests for clothes and other textiles. On the right of the lobby is the dwelling-room° with wood block floor, which served both as kitchen, living and bed-room for the family and has a raised open fireplace with chimney-crane° or movable bracket. There is a long bench° under the window and the long table at which the family and the servants took their meals together, the farmer sitting at the head of the table. By the box-bed is a warmingpan and the farmer's gun and powder-horn. In the corner is a dresser, hanging-shelves and a baby° walker. A door leads into a passage. To the left is the pantry, to the right the cobbled back-kitchen or scullery°, which served as bake and brew-house and in which the cooking was done during the summer. It has a raised hearth in the chimney with a bread° oven at the rear, a malt° kiln to the right and a fixed brewing copper to the left all of which are fired from the chimney. Implements for baking, brewing, butchering, and laundry work. In the corner by the table is a long cider-press. On the shelves under the ceiling are milk pans for skimming cream. Note on the shelves the unglazed black or grey pottery built up of coils of clay, a Funen° domestic industry. The door by the fixed° copper leads to the maidservant's room. In the west wing is the farm servant's room, cowshed and stable. To the north and east is a horse-mill, threshing-floor and barns. The garden south of the dwelling-house is typical of the period about 1775–1880 and is surrounded by a banked stone wall. The house belonged to the manor estate and was occupied by a tenant°.

Head° pad

Stand° for yeast

Malt frame to place under the filter when brewing

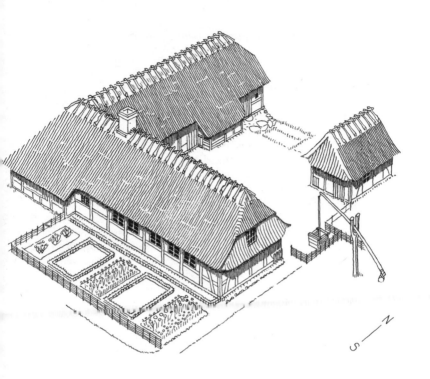

72. SMALLHOLDER'S FARMSTEAD FROM
DANNEMARE, LOLLAND

Built in the form of a right angle, the dwelling-house is to the south
and the covered gateway, barn and cowsheds to the west. In the
courtyard is a small separate building used as a workshop and to
house the geese. The walls and half-timbering° are whitewashed
and the roof is thatched. Crossing the garden and entering the
courtyard, there is a door on the east end of the dwelling-house

Bobbin°

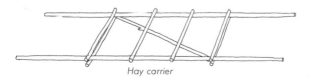

Hay carrier

leading to a small lobby. To the left is the "best° room", to the right the living room with its long table and long bench° placed against the partition wall in the medieval manner (see no. 54). After the introduction of glass windows, it became customary elsewhere in Denmark to put the table and bench° by the outside wall near the windows (see nos. 1, 63, 71). From the living-room a door leads into the kitchen, and from there out into the courtyard.

To the south of the covered gateway in the south wing are a threshing floor and a barn, and to the north another barn with hencoop and dog kennel. Beyond is the cowshed and sheep shed and in the outshot° in the courtyard is a pigsty.

Stand° for smoked bacon

Skin scraper

Buildings nos. 72–73 come from the flat fertile island of Lolland south of Zealand. The country people there were rather prosperous and their half-timbered° buildings with roofs of straw or reeds were more solid than those of Zealand. Close contact with the former Danish Duchy of Schleswig across the water has influenced the ground plans of the buildings; the dwelling-house is more closely connected to the farm buildings than in other parts of Denmark and there is a connecting door between them. In some cases the remains of very ancient forked uprights may be seen supporting the wall° plates (western outshot° in number 73). The medieval custom of placing the table and long bench° by the partition wall is still found (number 72).

Between nos. 72 and 73 is a **village° meeting place from Lolland** (see no. 69). The farmers sat on a circular platform of earth with a tree in the centre. The platform is supported on the outside by a wattle fence.

Village° meeting place

73. SMALLHOLDER'S FARMSTEAD FROM TÅGENSE, LOLLAND

A "longhouse"° with outhouse (cowshed etc.) in the western end and dwelling-house in the eastern. It is half-timbered°, white-washed, and has a thatched roof. The western gable end forms an outshot° made of large granite stones. The roof of this outshot is carried on tall uprights which are Y-shaped at the top. This primitive timber work is a legacy from prehistoric times while the main framework of the cottage is constructed in the style of village carpenters of about 1800. On the northern side there is a long outshot.

Hedging maul

In the outshot at the western end there is a pigsty and a bunker for fuel. Next to this is the barn with a stall for two cows and a hencoop in the corner, then the threshing-floor with winnowing machine. Beyond is the dwelling-house with an entrance lobby and beyond it a pantry. In the outshot is a larder. The living-room on the right has an iron stove° and four-poster° bed. There is a small kitchen with a raised hearth in the chimney fireplace and two bread° ovens

Dough trough

Yarn winder

Fulling board

Board for polishing knives

behind. The "best° room" is a later addition and has a bed for guests; it also contains weaving implements. Finally there is a workshop° for making tools and implements for the farm. Note the tiny ladder for the cat to climb up to the loft. Behind the cottage is a sweep well°. – The cottage had only a small amount of land, so that the smallholder earned his living by working for other farmers as well.

Shaving° horse

Pig killing bench

Sun-dried° brick mould

Forked upright carrying wall° plate

Half-timbering° with wattle° and daub

Round the neighbouring enclosures you will see **wattle fences** of upright stakes with thin branches woven between them. In the past such fences° were very common, especially for dividing the plough from the heath or pasture land in the days of the open fields.

74. POST MILL FROM KARLSTRUP, ZEALAND

(No admission)

Built about 1662 and partly reconstructed in 1763. The sails are of a later type and when working would be covered with canvas though originally the covering was of wood (see no. 9). The post mill takes its name from the big vertical post about which the whole mill could be revolved depending on the direction of the wind. It was turned from the ground by means of the "tailpole", i.e. the sloping beam which also serves as a ladder to the door on the first floor.

Windmills in Denmark were recorded as early as the 13th century and post mills are the oldest known type. Number 5 shows a later type.

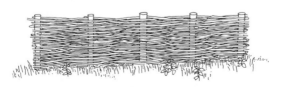

Wattle fence°

Glossary

Alcove bed: a bed built within the thickness of the wall, or in the out-shot, closed in with folding or sliding doors or with curtains. As was customary there is room for several people in it. It is short because they slept in a semi-sitting position. See Four° poster bed.

Baby walker: in which young children could be put to learn to walk. They were held securely below the armpits. There were different types – some taking the form of a bench with a sliding seat (no. 8) and others of a ring rotating round a bar fixed from the floor to the ceiling (no. 55).

Bacon rack, or stand for smoking bacon: a short, thick piece of wood with pegs set in it for hanging bacon, sausages, etc. while they were smoked in the chimney (no. 71). It could also take the form (no. 72) of a long pole reaching from the floor to the top of the open chimey with pegs in the upper end. See Open° chimney.

Bed wagon: for warming beds; a half cylindrical framework to hold a container of embers and hot ashes (no. 67). See Warming° pans.

Bench: in former times there was a traditional arrangement for the furniture in the dwelling-room° and most of it was fixed to the wall. There was always a long table in front of wall benches which were joined at the corner. Before the chimney was introduced, there was a flat open hearth in the middle of the floor. There were no windows but in the top of the roof there was a louver° or smoke-hole, so that daylight could only enter through the louver or the open door. Peasant houses were at that time so narrow that the long tables and benches had to be placed by one of the gable walls (no. 54). After the introduction of the chimney (from the seventeenth century onwards), a ceiling could be fitted and windows were put in the outer walls. The long tables and benches were then moved to the window wall and the benches arranged in the corner. There were traditional seats for the inhabitants of the house. The master's seat was always at the head of the table, and the sons and men-servants sat according to age and rank on the long bench below the windows, while the women stood or sat on seats without backs on the other side. Even if the room was not panelled there was always a wainscot behind the master's bench. The wainscot was as a rule beautifully carved or decorated with paintings (for example nos. 42 and 63).

Best room: a large room situated at one end of the house usually without chimney or stove°. It was only used for feasts and parties and for storing linen and clothes. The furniture is therefore mainly chests and cupboards but there was often a bed for guests. To protect the room against thieves, as it was rarely used, iron bars were often put in front of the windows. It also served the purpose of a box room for tools not in use and the loom stood there if there was no other room for it. Members of the family that died were laid out here before the funeral. Rich farms sometimes had two best rooms (nos. 34 and 71).

Bin: a large covered box in which corn, malt and flour were kept – often in the loft (in the lofts of nos. 63 and 71). Sometimes it took the form of a large round or oval straw° basket or was made of staves (like a barrel). In an earlier period they were also made of wattle° and daub.

Block for shaping woollen underpants: when a knitted article had been fulled it was placed on a block to prevent shrinking (no. 8). See Fulling° board.

Bobbin: there are two kinds of bobbin. The first is used to wind any kind of yarn which is then removed in a ball (no. 72). The second has a large round bottom with a thin stem above; the yarn was wound on the stem and a number of them were used for making round braid by plaiting the yarns together.

Brazier: portable flat iron container which was filled with embers for heating (no. 31). Sometimes a wooden barrel lined with clay was used. See Foot° warmer.

Bread oven: found in all farmsteads and in a number of smallholders' cottages. It was usually connected with an open fireplace in the scullery° (nos. 9, 40, 42, 67, 68 and 71), but in the kitchen (nos. 59 and 73) when there was only one chimney. In districts under Frisian influence a little bread oven might be found under the hearth (nos. 2 and 31). The great vaulted bread ovens of claystone or mud sometimes protruded outside the building under a lean-to° (nos. 59 and 68). A fire was made in the oven itself and afterwards the ashes were taken out with a rake and the loaves were placed in it with a spade-shaped wooden oven° peel (no. 55). The opening was normally covered with a wooden shutter coated with mud or in later years with an iron plate. A batch of ryeloaves lasted about six weeks. White bread was only made for feasts and festivals. On account of fire danger the bread oven was sometimes built outside in a small building by itself, which was sometimes jointly owned (no. 8). See Open° chimney.

Brick walls: walls of bricks and mortar were used in some stately buildings from c. 1160. They were not found until much later in peasant homes. The earliest brick built houses date from about 1600 in south-west Schleswig; from here they spread slowly north and were quite common in west Jutland (where there was little timber) after 1800. They appeared later still in the rest of Denmark. This country has no natural rock, only loose glacial boulders, so that stone was never used for peasant houses except sometimes in the latter half of the 19th cent. or on the Faeroe islands and Bornholm where there was abundant natural rock.

Butter mould: bell shaped, of turned wood. Butter made in this kind of mould was sold by the volume of the mould and not by weight (no. 31). Another form of mould was used for making a pattern on the butter.

Button mould: for casting metal buttons. It was usually cut from soft stone (no. 31).

Cake spit: for baking big pyramidal hollow cakes over an open fire. The dough is put on in layers and baked a little at a time while the spit is turned (no. 55).

Candle holder: a primitive candle stick in which the candle was held in a slip (no. 1).

Candle making: in former times the peasants made their own candles from tallow. In smaller households the melted tallow was poured into oval or oblong containers of wood or pottery (no. 68) into which the wicks were dipped several times between drying. The fatter the candle required, the more often it was dipped. Several wicks were dipped together and for the purpose were hung on a short stick which during drying was placed on a horizontal frame like a ladder. In bigger households a round candle table with a rotating top was used, and under the table top hung small round wooden discs with iron hooks for the wicks underneath (no. 42). These discs were dipped in tallow in a bucket shaped container. At a later date some peasants used candle moulds of tin or glass (no. 42).

Candlestand: a tall candlestick that stands on the floor. Several people could sit around it and work at night. The height was often adjustable (for example no. 71).

Cellar: in old peasant houses there was no cellar but only a larder with a sunk floor (no. 2). Cellars were only found in the wealthier farmhouses in some districts (no. 34 – constructed later than the house). In Eiderstedt in south-west Schleswig vaulted cellars were found from the seventeenth century (no. 31).

Cheese mould: the curd was poured in and pressed so that the whey ran out through the openings in the mould. A scrim was placed between the curd and the mould. Some moulds were wooden and were either square (no. 54) or round and could have a carved pattern in the base which was imprinted on the cheese. Others were made of pottery pierced at the bottom and called cheese cups, and some primitive ones were of coiled straw (no. 57). See Cheese° press, Straw° basket.

Cheese press: with one or more plungers for pressing the cheese in the mould (nos. 42 and 63). See Cheese° mould.

Chest of drawers: chests with lids began to be replaced in peasant homes by chests of drawers in the eighteenth century. There was also a transitional type with only one drawer.

Chimney-crane: an adjustable bracket for hanging kettles over the fire in the open° chimney. It consisted of a vertical iron bar with a horizontal arm which could be adjusted for height (nos. 42, 67, 68 and 70). In no. 4, next to the hearth, is a heavy wooden post which previously carried a chimney crane. See Ratchet° hanger.

Churn: early churns were of cylindrical coopered construction narrower at the top than the bottom. The butter was churned by the use of a stick with a frame on the end which was worked up and down inside the churn (no. 63). A later type of churn was box-shaped with rotating paddles inside turned by a handle (no. 55) or sometimes the box took the form of a cradle that was rocked to and from (no. 42).

Cider press: for squeezing the juice out of crushed apples or pears. The oldest known type consisted of a wooden frame approximately sex feet long with a semi-circular container made of spindles at one end; the fruit was placed in this in a sack. A wooden block was placed on top and this was forced down to squeeze out the juice by means of a beam pivotted at one end which was pulled down by a capstan at the far end of the frame (no. 71).

Clay knife: a curved blade used by the potter to cut clay from the lump (no. 43).

Clinker-built: boat construction in which the boards overlap unlike carvel-built boats in which they join edge to edge. Clinker construction dates in Scandinavia back to the Iron Age and is still used in smaller boats while in bigger ones it has been replaced by carvel-built construction (no. 9).

Collar beam: a tie beam connecting the rafters together in pairs but is not found when the roof is supported by ridge posts. See Rafter°, Tie° beam, Half-timbering°.

Coop: used for hatching out geese or hens but also as a bench° in the dwelling-room. There were sliding doors to close it in front.

Copper lustre: pottery with a copper coloured glaze was introduced from England (particularly Staffordshire and Sunderland) to Denmark in the first half of the nineteenth century (for example no. 42).

Cruck houses: with curved uprights which reach to the ridge°and act as rafters°; have not been found in Denmark but might have existed in older times. Small buildings are, however, found which consist of a pitched roof placed directly on the ground (no. 29). Cruck construction should not be confused with the type of ridge post° construction which has two inclining ridge posts from the ground to the ridge beam°. See Ridge° post.

Crusie lamp: usually a three-cornered iron bowl which was hung up and had a piece of rush marrow lying in one corner or in a spout as a wick. It was often provided with a larger container of similar shape to catch the drips (nos. 1 and 4).

Curfew: (from French **couvre feu**) a brass, iron or pottery cover to place over the hearth embers at night to prevent fire (no. 4). There were two forms; for use on the open hearth they were bell shaped but where there was a chimney a half round form was placed over the embers against the back wall. In Britain the term also came to mean the tolling of the evening bell as a signal that fires should be extinguished at the hour at which the curfew was rung.

Currier's iron: a curved iron bar fixed to a wall or a post through which wash leather was pulled a number of times in order to soften it (in the workshop of no. 9 and in the cowshed of no. 54). It could also be made of osiers.

Cutting wire: used by potters to cut a turned pot free from the wheel (no. 43).

Decoy swan: placed on the water in order to attract wild swans which were at one time killed and eaten (no. 9).

Dendrochronological dating: a method for dating buildings by measuring and comparing the annual growth rings in timber. The method is based on the fact that the width of the rings is influenced by the weather and other conditions of each different year. In favourable cases the exact year of the felling of a tree can be established.

Dinner pail for women during confinement: it was the custom for neighbours and friends to bring food to a woman who had just had a baby. This food, usually a fruit soup, was brought in a pottery jar, though it was sometimes made of brass. The same container was also used for sending food as a contribution to a party to which one had been invited (for example no. 68).

Distaff: holder for flax°, tow° or hemp which was placed on top of the spinning wheel, from which the raw material could be pulled while spinning (flax distaff no. 54, tow distaff no. 67).

Dwelling-room: usually heated with an iron stove°. It was formerly dining-room and bedroom as well and sometimes also kitchen; in the latter case there was an open° chimney (nos. 42, 54 and 71). This old form of house had as a rule only one dwelling-room, but bigger farms might have two (no. 42). In some districts there was one dwelling-room facing south for the winter and another for the summer facing north (nos. 2 and 34). There was a traditional way of furnishing the old peasant dwelling-room and most of the furniture was fixed to the wall. The beds were often alcove° beds. See Bench°.

Ember holder: hot embers were placed in the holder and taken from it with a pair of tongs in order to light a pipe (no. 1).

Feed rack: a frame hung up to hold hay or straw which cattle and sheep can eat by pulling it through the bars (no. 31).

Fences: formerly used to divide the ploughland from the heath or pasture in the days of open fields. Sometimes they were wattle fences consisting of upright stakes with thin branches woven between them (nos. 71, 73 and 74). Others were wider, being made of two lines of stakes filled in the middle with brushwood (north of no. 29). Such fences used a great quantity of stakes and brushwood as they only lasted a few years; as a result the woodlands suffered. After the improvement of agriculture at the turn of the nineteenth century such fences were replaced by stone walls or earth banks.

Fiery cross: in some districts, to summon members of a village community to a meeting, a wooden or iron emblem known as a fiery cross or bode stick was sent round the village. In most districts, however, the members were summoned by blowing a horn. The fiery cross was also used to summon men to arms in the middle ages. In Scotland a fiery cross, usually burning at one end and dipped in blood at the other to symbolize the fire and the sword, was used to summon the clans. See Village° community.

Fixed copper: see Scullery°, Hops°.

Flail: for threshing corn. It consisted of a hand staff and a beater joined by a strap of leather or eelskin. The sheaves were spread out on the threshing floor and beaten with the flail so that the grain was separated from the ears (no. 63). This method has been replaced by threshing machines and was only used in later years for threshing straw required for thatching.

Flax: up to the end of the nineteenth century flax was grown in some districts for home use. After harvest, the seed pods were removed with a tool rather like a thatcher's° comb (no. 62). Then the flax was wetted and dried artificially. The woody parts were now brittle and to help in removing them the stalks were broken in a flax braker (no. 63). An older and more primitive tool for this purpose was a round club (no. 54). To complete the removal of the woody parts a handful of flax was then held in a flax scutcher and beaten with a flat bat (nos. 67 and 65); alternatively it could be beaten while being held on the back of a chair. The woody material and broken flax removed in this process were known as flax tow. The remaining long soft flax fibres were then carded (for example no. 42) ready for spinning into thread or yarn which was made into linen.

Fleam: for bleeding animals, particularly horses, and usually kept at the village smithy. Horses were bled when they suffered from a variety of ailments and sometimes when they were not ill at all – for example to lower the high spirits of stallions in the spring. The blade of the fleam was hammered into a vein with the fleam stick (no. 70).

Floor sand: used for sprinkling on mud floors and on scrubbed deal floors (soft wood) so that dust and dirt could be swept away more easily. There was often a special box or cupboard for the sand (for example no. 63).

Folding bed: a bench or sofa the seat of which can be opened up and a drawer beneath pulled out so that one or more – particularly children – can sleep on it (for example nos. 8, 22, 59 and 70).

Foot-warmer: a closed portable container for embers, often a pierced box of brass or wood with an earthen pot inside for the embers (no. 4). It could be placed under a woman's skirts. In former times tripod pots of brass or pottery, or wooden tubs lined with mud, were used. Square warming° pans of iron on four legs were also used as portable heaters. See Brazier°.

Four poster bed: a bed with tall posts at the corners or high panels at the ends, which support a canopy from which hang curtains that can be drawn. Sometimes there are no posts and the curtains hang from a moulding under the ceiling. There were other different forms but all of them had some kind of superstructure over the bed. The beds were often broad enough to accommodate several people and short because they slept in a semi-sitting position. See Alcove° bed.

Fulling board: a corrugated board on which newly woven woollen cloth was thickened after treatment with hot soapy water. This made the woollen cloth thicker and stronger (no. 73). More primitive fulling° boards consisted of wattle frames (no. 63). See Block° for shaping woollen underpants.

Funen pottery: coarse, black (occasionally reddish), unglazed pottery previously made in the home by women in some districts on the island of Funen. A very ancient technique was used in which long round clay rolls were formed by hand and put together in a spiral to make a pot. A potter's wheel was not used but the pot was built up on a stand something like that used by a sculptor for modelling and turned slowly by hand. The pots were fired without any air in pits rather like Jutland° pots or as in very primitive kilns (nos. 68, 70 and 71). See Jutland° pottery.

Gingerbread mould: a short board with figures carved in it (no. 31). The design shows Dutch influence.

Glazing stone: a round stone (sometimes glass) with one side flat and the other convex used for glazing starced linen. It could also be used as a pestle to crush spices, etc. Such stones usually lay on the stove and could thus be used as hand warmers.

Ground plate: a long horizontal piece of timber which forms the bottom member of the frame in half-timbered° buildings and which rests on the ground° sill and into which the uprights are mortised (for example nos. 4, 42 and 67). In districts where timber was scarce there is no ground plate and the uprights are placed directly on the ground sill (nos. 1, 8 and 9). See Ground° sill, Half-timbering°.

Ground sill: the name given to the foundation stones which formed the base of the walls in earlier peasant houses. They were not set in mortar but rested on the earth. See Ground° plate.

Half-timbering: the outer and inner walls consist of a framework of timber and the space between is filled in with wattle° and daub, or in later years occasionally with sun-dried° or real bricks°. The timber of the outer walls is nearly always oak but the beams are of pine. The drawing shows the more highly developed form (for example nos. 42, 67, 68 and 71) in which the beams are mortised through the upright posts. In some districts of Zealand they are sometimes mortised into the side of the upright posts (no. 62). About 1800 in peasant houses it became usual to place the tie° beams on top of the wall or the wall° plate (for example nos. 8 and 70), but this technique was used much earlier in town houses and manor houses. The fully developed half-timbering as shown in the drawing results from the influence of carpenters from the towns. An older way of building partly inherited from prehistoric times is now and then to be found as a survival in primitive country half-timbering. In this case the upright posts were sometimes dug into the ground and often finished at the top in a Y-shaped fork on which the wall° plate or the ends of the beams rested (the lean-to° at the gables of nos. 60 and 73 and the shed no. 63). Where there was not much timber available, the construction was simpler than in the drawing. In its most simple form the half-timbering consisted merely of upright posts and the horizontal wall° plate resting on top of the wall supporting the rafters°. In such cases there is no ground° plate on the foundation stones as the posts rest directly on the stones themselves (no. 1, intermediate forms nos. 8, 60, 61 and 63; the last three houses from Zealand have only short pieces of timber on the foundation stones between the upright posts). A special type of construction is found in buildings with ridge° posts rising from the ground (nos. 67 and 71) or in buildings composed of a nave and two side aisles (nos. 1 and 4). Some buildings have outshots° (nos. 62, 63 and 73). Buildings with horizontal heavy boards placed between upright posts are related to half-timbering (nos. 37–40, 54 and 55). Two-storied peasant houses were not known until the nineteenth century in Denmark. See Wattle° and daub, Ridge° post, Oak° houses.

Hames: two long curved pieces of wood which are attached to each side of the collar round an animal's neck when harnessing it for draught. The trace chains from the implement are then attached to the hooks on the hames. See Ox° collar.

Hand harrow: a long handle with some short twigs or mortised prongs inserted vertically near the end, used to rake in the seed which was broadcast on land which had been cleared for cultivation by paring off the heather or cutting and burning the trees and scrub (no. 54).

Hand mills: in more recent times used mainly for grinding malt for brewing beer and only occasionally for grinding corn as the stones were too light and rotated too slowly to grind fine flour (for example no. 63). Before grain could be ground it had to be dried artificially. In smaller homes this was usually done in wooden trays or drawers on the iron stove° in the dwelling-room° (nos. 1 and 9) or in the bread° oven after it had been used for baking.

Hanging cupboard: a small cupboard which usually hung in the corner at the end of the table behind the master's seat. In it important papers and other valuables were kept.

Harvest barrel: a small barrel or costrel for keeping beer in when working in the fields. The barrel has two holes, one for drinking out of and the other for letting air in. It was particularly common to use them at harvest time but they were used at other times of the year as well (no. 68).

Hay gaff: used for pulling hay or straw out of the building in which it is stored (no. 9).

Head pad: a padded wreath covered with bright coloured cloth for carrying milk buckets on the head. After milking in the fields the women brought the buckets of milk back in this way (no. 71).

Heddle loom: for weaving narrow braid. It is usually formed of a piece of board with holes and slits alternating. One thread of the warp is passed through a hole and the next through a slit and so on. When the heddle is lifted or lowered the weft, on a small flat shuttle, can be passed between the two levels of the warp. The warp was attached at one end to a firm object such as the window sill and at the other to the waist of the worker (for example no. 34). In some districts a more complicated braiding loom was used (nos. 42 and 54).

Hip-roof: a roof that in addition to sloping down to the two side walls also slopes to the gable wall (nos. 4 and 8). When half-hipped the gable wall continues further up before the slope starts (nos. 1 and 67). A hipped roof is less susceptible to wind damage than an upright gable. Hipping is, therefore, to be found in windswept areas such as West Jutland.

Hops: when beer was home brewed, a fixed° copper for brewing was nearly always found in the kitchen or scullery. As early as 1500, because of the demand for hops° for brewing, farmers were compelled to plant them. It was often difficult to find long, straight hop poles for the fir tree did not become common in Denmark until the nineteenth century. The usual way of supporting them was therefore to let the hop bine grow up straw ropes stretched from the ground to a star-shaped wooden framework which was supported by a single central pole. On the island of Funen home brewing and hop growing continued until modern times and hops were sold to other parts of Denmark (nos. 67 and 71).

Ice shoes: overshoes of wood with iron nails underneath for walking on ice, for example when fishing (no. 34).

Juniper mill: in some districts juniper was used to flavour beer or spirits. For this purpose it had to be crushed in a mill (no. 54).

Jutland pottery: pots of many different shapes for cooking and other uses made of unglazed black or grey clay. They were made by women in some rural districts of Jutland – often in the farmsteads. The technique appears to be a continuation of that used in the iron age. The pots were shaped without a wheel by hollowing and shaping a piece of clay by hand; the curving sides were produced by pressure from the inside. The only tools used were scrapers and knives, smooth round stones and a wet cloth for smoothing. After drying the pots were treated in smoke and finally fired with heather turf at a rather low temperature stacked in an airtight pit out of doors. Jutland pots were formerly sold all over Denmark and exported to neighbouring countries as well: production only began to decrease in the second half of the nineteenth century (for example nos. 1, 2, 8. 9. 22, 31 and 34). See Funen° pottery.

Lean-to or outshot: a narrow low extension from the nave° of the building which forms a side aisle and over which the main roof projects. See Nave° and side aisle construction.

Log house: the walls were built of horizontal heavy poles usually of pine. The ends of these trunks in each layer project and are groove jointed at the corners. The length of every house depends on the length of the poles. As the corner joints bind the walls, tie° beams are not necessary (nos. 56, 57, 58 and the dwelling house of no. 54). The Scandinavians appear to have learnt to build log houses in the Viking Age when crossing Russian rivers. Such buildings became common in Sweden and Norway but no traces of them have so far been found in Denmark.

Long house: a building consisting of several bays built end to end without any wings. It represents a very ancient house type and is often found in smallholders' cottages. Such buildings were often quite long and contained both the dwelling house and the farm buildings (for example nos. 1, 2, 60, 61 and 73).

Louver: an outlet for smoke in the roof used in conjunction with an open hearth prior to the introduction of chimneys (no. 1). Louvers were common in prehistoric times and were not superseeded in Danish peasant houses until the sixteenth and seventeenth centuries; even after this they remained in use in some poorer districts until the nineteenth century. Where there was a louver it was not possible to have a ceiling and loft but in some districts a loft was built and the smoke was led up to it by three walls built on the hearth; this represented an intermediate stage in the development of the chimney (no. 9). See Open° chimney.

Lynch pin: a small wedge-shaped iron pin which is put through the end of the axle to keep the wheel in place. In Denmark the lynch pin has often a curved flat head to prevent dirt from falling into the axle box. (Waggons with lynch pins in nos. 31, 42, 63 and 71). As wooden axles were later replaced by iron ones, lynch pins were replaced by box nuts.

Malt kilns: for drying malt, which was to be used for brewing beer. While drying, the malt was placed on pieces of wickerwork or on wooden boards. The malt kiln was stood in an open° chimney and the malt containers were placed higher up in the chimney after which the opening was closed with a large hatch (no. 71). In smaller households the malt was dried on a tray or in a drawer on the iron stove° (nos. 1 and 9), or even in the bread° oven after baking. Sometimes the malt kilns were placed in small separate sheds because of fire danger.

Mangle board: for mangling linen. The linen was wound on a wooden roller which was rolled along the table under pressure from the board. The boards were often decorated with carving or colours which incorporated the initials of the woman who owned it. The handle was often shaped like a horse (for example no. 1).

Mark: usually a runic sign used instead of a written name to indicate either the name of a man or his property. Every peasant had his own mark for marking his cattle and tools, etc. It was also used as a signature by people who could not write. The mark was normally of a design that could easily be carved on wood.

Marline-spike: shaped like a big bodkin; it was used for splicing ropes (no. 2).

Mobile: for hanging under the ceiling. It was often made of straw but might also take the form of a carved wooden bird similar to the dove of the Holy Ghost found in churches.

Mustard grinder: mustard sauce was eaten a great deal especially with fish. The mustard was ground either in a small hand mill (no. 42) or in a bowl with a heavy ball of iron or stone (no. 55).

Nave and side aisle construction: in some Jutland districts this type of construction is found in half-timbered° houses. What, in ordinary buildings, would be the roof-bearing outer walls are here replaced by two rows of inner uprights into which the beams are mortised. These uprights support a horizontal wall° plate on which the rafters° are placed. The roof projects on both sides over narrow side aisles or outshots° to the low outer walls. The main construction is thus well protected against the weather. The side aisles were used for small rooms and alcove° beds or as a larder; sometimes there was no dividing wall and the outshot° remained open to the nave (nos. 1, 4, 22 and 25). See Lean-to° or outshot, Wall° plate, Tie° beam, Rafters°.

Oak house: houses built entirely of oak were once rather common in Denmark, especially in the wooded districts. The walls are constructed of heavy horizontal boards with the ends mortised into the dividing uprights (nos. 37–40, 55 and the outhouses no. 54).

Open chimney: a chimney which is broad at the bottom and open along the front giving the appearance of a high fireplace. The food was prepared on a raised stone hearth which either covered the whole floor area of the chimney (for example nos. 9, 31, 42, 67, 68 and 71) or one side of it (for example nos. 59, 61, 62, 63 and 73). In the last houses (nos. 63 and 73) the person cooking actually stood inside the chimney. An open fire burnt on top of the platform and the pots were hung over it on ratchet° hangers or placed on iron trivets. Draught holes were not introduced until the nineteenth century (nos. 9 and 31) and later still the iron kitchen range became common (no. 6). At the sides and back of the open chimney various stoves° or ovens could be built and they were stoked through openings in the chimney walls (for example bread° ovens, fixed° coppers in the scullery° and an iron stove° in the dwelling-room° or a malt°

kiln). In some districts there was only one chimney in the house which was in the kitchen or kitchen-living room but in others there was also one in the scullery°. See Ratchet° hanger, Stove°, Bread° oven, Louver°.

Outshot: see Lean-to°.

Oven peel: see Bread° oven.

Over-shoe: placed on the hooves of horses when they had to walk in boggy meadows or marsh, thus increasing the area of contact with the ground (no. 8).

Ox collar: a collar made of rush or straw which was put round the neck of the animal and to which the hames° were fastened (no. 8). A similar collar was used for horses. See Hames°.

Pepper grinder: for grinding or pounding pepper or spices. Some were attached to the table by a wooden thumb screw (for example no. 71) while others were goblet shaped and free-standing (no. 42). In both types the grinding was done with a pestle.

Pine light holder: for holding a burning splint of resinous pine for light (nos. 54 and 55).

Platter: wooden plates were once much used and were usually round or square and flat. Sometimes they were very long and could reach along the table to serve two or three people. Platters were mainly used for bacon and salted herrings which were both common dishes. Occasionally a slice of ryebread was used as a plate.

Porringer: a round dish of pewter or pottery with a lip under the outer brim. Several people sitting round the table could eat with spoons from the same dish.

Potato grater: used to make potato flour (no. 54).

Primitive spear: made from an old scythe blade mounted on a long handle and used by peasant for self-protection or when drafted into the militia. Such implements were common centuries ago but were used as recently as 1807 to fight the British when they landed after the bombardment of Copenhagen while the Danish army was in Schleswig-Holstein (no. 71).

Pug mill: to prepare raw clay for use by the potter or the brickmaker it has to be carefully worked to give it a smooth consistency. The primitive way of doing this is with the feet but since the nineteenth century it has been common to use a special mill for the purpose called a pug mill. In no. 43 the mill consists of a spiral auger driven by a horse. The clay is fed in at the top.

Pyramid shelves: triangular wall shelves, often decorated, which were much used in peasant dwelling-rooms° for tea cups and knick-knacks, etc.; they were sometimes placed on the top of a chest° of drawers (no. 4).

Rafters: in Danish the word indicates very primitive rafters, that is, laths and sticks which run from the top of the wall to a ridge° beam and are not held together by means of tie° beams. In buildings with turf roofs they are close together. Such rafters are only found in primitive houses for they were later replaced with heavier rafters with tie° beams. In roof construction using ridge posts from the ground the rafters ride on a ridge pole and rest loosely on and over the outer walls (nos. 67 and 71). See Ridge° post.

Rape fork: rape or coleseed (Brassica napus) was grown extensively for the oil that could be extracted from its seed which was sold to oil mills. The oil was used for burning in lamps and for making into soap. The fork was used for collecting the rape at harvest time which had to be carefully treated to avoid loss of seed. It was then threshed on a big cloth in the field by a heavy horsedrawn roller (no. 31).

Ratchet hanger: for hanging cooking pots over the fire in the open° chimney. It was provided with ratchet teeth so that the height could be adjusted (for example no. 62). See Open° chimney, Chimney° crane.

Rattle: such rattles were used among other purposes for calling cattle home or for scaring wandering cattle away from the corn fields (no. 9).

Restraining yoke for sheep: to couple two sheep together – for example to milk them or to keep a ram and a ewe apart (no. 31). See Sheep° restrainer.

Ridge: the thatched roof sides join together at the ridge° and thus need special covering. In some districts a layer of straw or seaweed is placed on the ridge and this layer is kept in place with a row of roof-trees° of Λ-shaped cross-pieces of wood sitting over it. In other districts the ridge is covered with turf.

Ridge beam: a pole lying horizontally under the ridge supporting the top ends of the rafters. In ridge° post construction the ridge beam is particularly heavy because the rafters° ride on it without tie° beams (no. 71). In roofs made of grass sods or turf there is a heavy ridge beam and a side beam or purlin half way down either side of the roof. On top of these are placed rafters° upon which the turf rests (nos. 54, 56 and 57). See Rafters°, Ridge° post.

Ridge post: a high post through the middle of the house supporting the ridge° beam on which the rafters° of the roof ride. In some Danish districts the original type of ridge post which rests on the ground is still to be found, while in Great Britain they start from the beams (king posts). Very old ridge posts have a y-shaped top for carrying the ridge° beam; later, however, they were mortised. In this construction there is no tie° beam between the rafters° (the outhouses in nos. 54 and 71). In districts where flimsier pinewood was used for want of oak the uprights were alternated with inclined posts. This construction is not to be mistaken for the cruck° construction found in Britain. See Cruck° houses.

Roof-trees: see Ridge°.

Rope hook for wagon: when a wagon had been loaded with sheaves of corn at harvest a long pole was put on top of the load and secured at the front by a rope. Another rope from the back of the pole was then pulled tight round the rope hook and tied (no. 63).

Salt trough: for salting bacon and meat. They were once made from a hollowed tree trunk rather like a dug-out canoe (no. 68).

Sausage filler: rings sawn from a cow horn which were used for filling sausage meat into the skins (no. 42).

Scullery: a large room for washing, brewing, slaughtering and baking. In it were normally found a fixed° copper, bread° oven and perhaps malt° kiln (no. 71). These were stoked from a big open° chimney or if there was only one chimney in the house from the kitchen hearth (nos. 59, 61 and 63). The scullery also contained many tools used in these and other household tasks. It was as a rule situated in a gable end of the house with a door to the yard; occasionally it was a separate building (no. 55). See Open° chimney.

Scythe and gathering stick: a short scythe (sometimes known as a Hainault scythe) which was used together with a short stick which had an iron hook at the end. The harvester held the scythe in his right hand while he gathered the corn with the stick in his left hand. The tool is named after the province of Hainault from which it originated on the borders of France and Belgium and it spread from there to other parts of north-western Europe such as the peninsula of Eiderstedt in south-west Schleswig (no. 31).

Scythe sharpening anvil: when scythes were made of wrought iron they were sharpened by tapping the edge of the blade with the narrow side of a hammer. In order to do this a small anvil was fixed to a special bench or to a block of wood (no. 8).

Seaweed roofs: near the coast the ridges of thatched roofs are often covered over with seaweed. On the island of Læsø, however, and in some districts on the east coast of Jutland the roofs were once covered entirely with seaweed which could be as much as three feet thick and lasted a very long time. In order to hold the seaweed on the roof in position, large pear-shaped rolls with long tails were attached to the lower laths and hung over the eaves being packed tightly together with smaller rolls between them. These hung over the wall of the house and made a firm foundation for the layers of seaweed which were then placed over the remainder of the roof. Several hundred cartloads of seaweed were required to cover such a roof as that of no. 9. The ridge° was very wide and was finished by covering with sods of turf.

Sewing cushion: for screwing to the edge of a table. The work could be pinned to the cushion to hold it in place while sewing (no. 8).

Shaving horse: a bench which has at one end a vice to hold wooden articles, such as clogs, while they are being shaped or worked on. The worker sits astride the bench (hence the name horse) and with his feet presses a treadle which by lever action grips the work (for example no. 73).

Sheep restrainer: to prevent grazing sheep (or cattle or horses) from running away or breaking through fences. Some took the form of wooden frames around the neck (no. 34) while other types included a stick hung under the neck by a chain or rope (no. 31).

Sickle: for cutting corn at harvest. In Denmark it was replaced by the scythe. In later years however, it was used for cutting rape (no. 34). See Rape° fork.

Sieve holder: a thin wooden frame on which a sieve could be stood over a bowl (no. 63).

Skimming pans: flat round dishes of clay or coopered wood, though in later times often of tinned iron. The milk stood in the pan while the cream rose. The pans stood on a shelf under the scullery° ceiling (no. 71) or in winter in the warm dwelling-room° (for example no. 63). Some farms had special milk larders or milk cupboards (nos. 6 and 34).

Skin scraper or Crotch stake: a spade shaped tool used for scraping skins while dressing them (no. 72).

Slip horn: a cow horn used by potters for decorating the pottery with slip or liquid clay (no. 43). Sometimes it was made of pottery.

Stand for yeast: a circular framework made of small pieces of wood, on which the yeast was placed to keep dry until the next brewing (no. 71). In a more primitive form it was made of plaited twigs.

Stilt: used by a potter for placing between glazed articles in the kiln to separate the surfaces (no. 43).

Stove: introduced in wealthier homes in Denmark at the end of the fifteenth century. The first ones were built of earthen pots or concave tiles°. In the late sixteenth century the iron stove was introduced. The oldest type was box shaped and it was fitted in the dwelling-room° in such a position that it could be stoked through the wall from the open° chimney in the kitchen. From the eighteenth century onwards the most common type had its own flue and was self-contained. Most peasants retained earthenware stoves of Jutland° pot and only the wealthier could afford iron stoves before the nineteenth century. See Open° chimney, Jutland° pottery.

Straw basket: container made of coiled straw work. The straw is made into bands by pressing it through an iron ring or a section of cow's horn. The bands are the sewn together with split willow or similar material. Such containers were used for storing many kinds of materials among them grain, flour and hops. Even large articles such as cradles, easy chairs and coffins could be made of straw (nos. 1 and 60). See Straw° rope.

Straw rope: ropes of straw were formerly much in use, for instance to fasten thatched roofs and for chair seats. Coils of especially thick straw rope could be used in walls and especially in the upper gables where they were wedged between wooden laths (no. 60). See Straw° basket.

Sugar cutters: they were either shaped like a pair of tongs and held in the hand (no. 70) or had much broader jaws and were fixed to the table edge (no. 34).

Sun-dried bricks: unfired bricks°, usually made by the peasants themselves in brick moulds (no. 73). They were only used for inside walls or for outer walls which were whitewashed or covered with reeds.

Tallow squeezer: two flat pieces of wood hinged at one end with which tallow could be compressed into a convenient space for transport (no. 31). A similar type was used for wax.

Taper holder: the taper was wound round the stem and held in the burning position by a pair of spring jaws at the top (no. 71).

Tenants: lords of manors let their farms and smallholdings to tenants who paid annual rent in kind and kept the buildings in repair. In addition they had to work on the manor farm. Before the condition of the peasantry was improved by law at the end of the eighteenth century, tenants were much worse off than freeholders and suffered bad conditions. In Zealand and Lolland-Falster peasants were attached to the soil and therefore compelled to reside in the place of their birth from the middle ages until 1788. In the rest of Denmark this was also the case from 1733–1788 but for military reasons.

Thatcher's bat: with which thatch was beaten into position in the roof (no. 62).

Thatcher's comb: the end was pushed into a hole in the wall to keep it in position and straw for thatching was then combed through the teeth to prepare it for use (no. 62).

Tie beams: long pieces of timber which cross the building from outer wall to outer wall and help to prevent the walls from sliding outwards from the pressure of the roof. The ends of the beams are either mortised through the uprights of the half-timbering° or rest upon the wall° plate of the outer wall. In peasant houses the latter construction did not become common until the early nineteenth century. In some districts of Zealand the beams are let into one side of the uprights (no. 62). See Half-timbering°, Wall°plate, Collar° beam.

Tiles: tin-glazed and decorated faience tiles from Dutch and particularly Frisian factories were commonly used along the North Sea coast in South Jutland and Schleswig for mounting on the walls in dwelling-rooms°. They helped to insulate the outer walls against damp and the chimney walls against tarry soot but were also decorative and were sometimes used for the top of small tea-tables (nos. 2, 4, 9, 31 and 34). Such tiles were also made on a small scale in Denmark.

Tinder box: for making fire. A steel was struck against a piece of flint and the sparks set fire to some tinder, which might have been dried fungus, touchwood or charred linen. Portable tinder boxes were carried in purses or small metal boxes while larger oblong ones, which sometimes had the steel mounted on a see-saw, were kept for household use (no. 60).

Tow: the coarser part of flax° or hemp which was removed in the process of hackling (carding). Yarn spun of flax tow was used for coarse cloth and yarn of hemp tow for, among other things, rope. See Flax°.

Twig for decorating pots: a small green twig with a smaller branch at one end. It was used for making dotted lines on pottery. When the point was placed against a rotating pot on the potter's wheel it made a border of small dots. It was sometimes made from a goose feather or a piece of wire (no. 43).

Village community: in the days of open field farming the farmers of a village formed a local organization or village meeting whose warden changed every year. At their meetings they took decisions about the timing of farm work and other matters affecting the welfare of the village; all farm work had to be carried out to a schedule agreed by these meetings. The community was bound both in its work and behaviour by a series of traditions which had the force of regulations and which in some instances can be traced back to the medieval guilds. Even petty crime could be brought for judgement to such a meeting rather than to the courts. Transgressors were fined and the proceeds of fines were used to pay for beer to be drunk at the annual festivals. The meetings took place in the open at the village meeting place usually on the village green for which purpose there was often a ring of stones under a lime tree where every farmer had his own stone to sit on (no. 69). In some districts instead of stones there was a flat mound (no. 72). The warden summoned a meeting by blowing a cow horn or less commonly by beating a drum or sending around a fiery cross or bode stick. See Fiery° cross.

102

Wall plate: a piece of timber lying horizontally on the top of the outer wall under the roof. In half-timbered° houses the uprights are mortised into the wall plate. In houses with side aisles the wall plate rests upon the inner uprights (no. 1). See Tie° beams, Nave° and side aisle construction.

Warming pans: of copper or brass with a perforated lid a long handle used to warm beds. They were filled with embers and warm ashes (no. 2). See Bed° wagon.

Washing bat: after clothes had been washed in lye (an alkaline detergent solution usually made from wood ash) they were rinsed and beaten with a wooden bat. Like mangle° boards these were often carved (for example no. 71).

Wattle and daub: between the wall timbers in half-timbered° houses there were vertical sticks interwoven with horizontal sticks. On to this framework there was placed from both sides a layer of clay mixed with sand which was smoothed and then coated with a thin layer of clay thinned with water. Finally, the walls were whitewashed or covered with reeds (in the east wing of nos. 63 and 68 a half-finished portion of the woven framework and clay can be seen on an inner wall). In some districts the clay was only applied to vertical sticks with or without plaited bands of straw or seaweed (to be seen in the south-west corner of no. 42 and in the workshop of no. 9). Wattle and daub was already in use in primitive huts in the stone age. See Half-timbering°.

Wells: there were two main kinds of wellhead. The one known as a winch well (for example no. 1) had a simple winch mechanism to raise the bucket. The other called a sweep well (for example no. 72) had a long sweep or beam pivotted in an upright at the side of the well. One end of the sweep had a long pole attached with the bucket on the end and the other was weighted to counterbalance the bucket.

Wheelwright (no. 61): the hub was first shaped roughly with an ax and then turned on the lathe. The holes for the spokes were then made in the hub and the spokes shaped with an ax, drawshave and plane. The spokes were fixed into the hub while it stood on a hub cradle, a special low bench on which it was held by wooden clamps. The rim of the wheel was made of six sections called felloes, which were sawn out with a bow saw – a type that could follow a curve – and then they were finished by planing with a special hollow plane. The felloes were then placed one at a time on a felloe horse, and the holes drilled for the spokes. After this the hub with the spokes in it was placed in the hub cradle, and the six felloes were fixed on the spokes. The hole for the bush and a axle was then drilled through the hub with an auger, which could be adjusted to make bigger or smaller holes. The finished wheel was then sent to the smith who fixed an iron tyre around it, or in former days not a complete tyre but iron strakes over the joints.

Wooden tray: an oblong wooden tray with fairly high sloping sides which was mainly used for the requirements of newly-born babies but also for lace, ribbons, etc. for women's headgear. They were usually carved and painted and carried the initials of the owner (no. 2). They were fashionable in the seventeenth century in Britain and were sometimes beautifully embroidered with beadwork or appliqué on wire gauze. They were called layette trays.

Wooden trivet: made of a V-shaped piece of wood on three short legs It was used to stand tubs on when washing or brewing (no. 63).

Workshop: before the modern age most tools and utensils were made at home by the farmer as far as possible from materials obtained on the farm or in the locality. Most farms therefore had a workshop in which such work could be done.

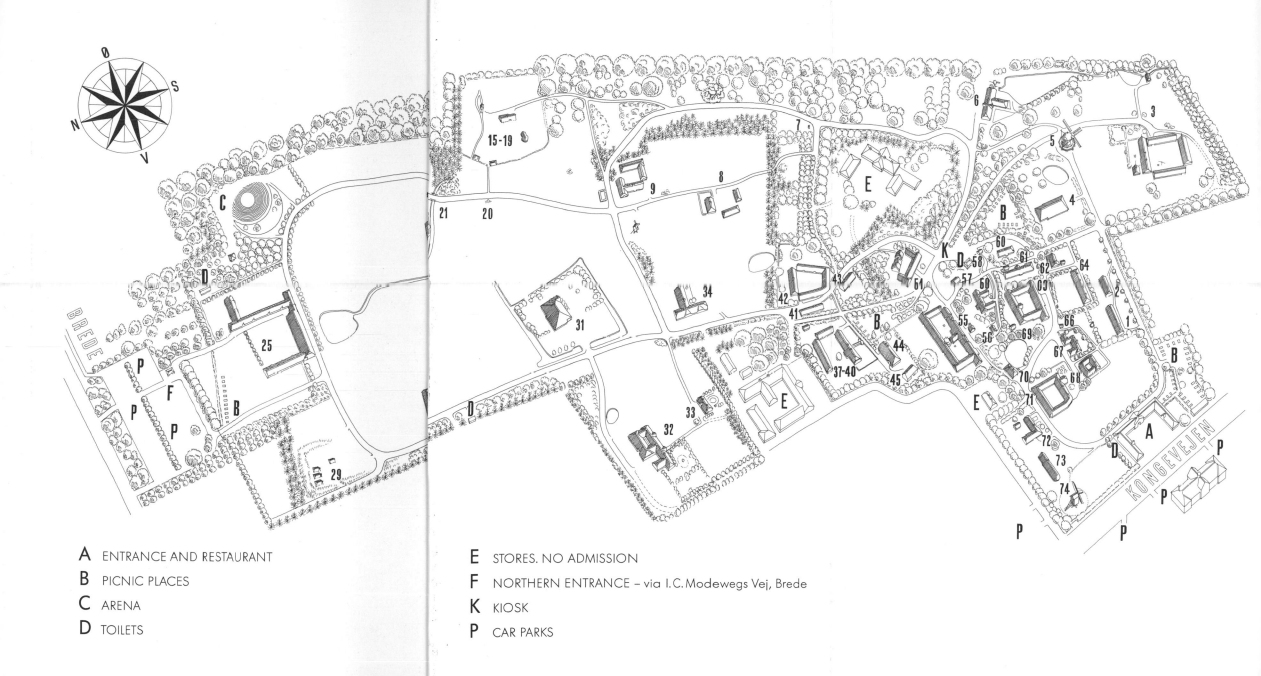

A ENTRANCE AND RESTAURANT

B PICNIC PLACES

C ARENA

D TOILETS

E STORES. NO ADMISSION

F NORTHERN ENTRANCE – via I.C. Modewegs Vej, Brede

K KIOSK

P CAR PARKS